Buster's
Secret Diaries

Buster's
Secret Diaries

As discovered by Roy Hattersley

Weidenfeld & Nicolson

LONDON

First published in Great Britain in 2007
by Weidenfeld & Nicolson

1 3 5 7 9 10 8 6 4 2

Text © Roy Hattersley 2007
Illustrations © John Ireland 2007

A CIP catalogue record for this book
is available from the British Library.

ISBN 97 8 02978 5216 2

Printed in Great Britain by Butler & Tanner Ltd,
Frome and London

Weidenfeld & Nicolson

The Orion Publishing Group Ltd
Orion House
5 Upper Saint Martin's Lane
London, WC2H 9EA

The Orion publishing group's policy is to use papers that
are natural, renewable and recyclable products and made
from wood grown in sustainable forests. The logging and
manufacturing processes are expected to conform to the
environmental regulations of the country of origin.

www.orionbooks.co.uk

Buster's
Secret Diaries

Author's Note

The story, which began in an overgrown Paddington yard, back in 1995, is not yet over. Much has changed with the passage of the years. I am wiser as well as older – not only whiter round the muzzle and longer in the tooth, but also a little less likely to leap without looking. In Derbyshire, where I spend half my life, I am still able to jump up to the window in the door, like a ferocious jack-in-the-box, when the postman knocks. And I still leap over the sofa into the drawing room when The Man who lives with me decides that, for the good of the postman, we are better kept apart. I still bare my teeth with bogus menace, but I go willingly. I now accept my temporary exile from the hall with tail held high and confidence that, in five minutes, I shall be back where I belong.

The Man has grown old too, but less gracefully. And, if our walks are any guide, he is not as fit as I am. Unlike me, he has not looked after himself. I eat a carefully balanced diet, drink only water, take regular exercise and have my teeth cleaned every night. All I can be sure about him is that he cleans his teeth. But although he finds difficulty in negotiating stiles, which I bound over in one leap (unless it is cold weather and my joints are stiff), he still hobbles along at the other end of the lead. And my feelings about him are the same as they were on that December night when he found me in a basket outside the bedroom door. I knew straight away that he was not just for Christmas, but for life.

I knew that we would be friends as soon as he knelt down beside me and rubbed behind my ears like a man who knew about dogs and wanted to make them happy. And he was very good about the vomit. It was barely on the hall floor before he said that it did not matter. Since then I have been sick dozens of times, usually in inconvenient places. But The Man always says that terriers behave like that and cheerfully cleans it up without complaint.

I think that The Man is kind by nature – a characteristic I admire without wanting to exhibit it myself. But he is also immensely competitive. He takes credit for the achievements of others – particularly mine. Whenever he introduces me to a new acquaintance, he always says, 'Buster lived wild for six months, but he's a friendly enough chap now. A bit difficult at first, but love and bribery did the trick.' The clear implication is that he tamed me. This is not true. I tamed myself.

When the canine care home was trying to get me adopted, they told people I 'lacked social skills with both people and dogs'. That was true. Now, you could take me (almost) anywhere. Then, the best that the dog adoption agency could say about me was that I was 'very clean'. That was true as well. But there was far more to recommend me than that. Without strength of character and indomitable courage I would never have survived.

Once upon a time, I listened to the wolf who lives inside my head. He is still there. But now, for most of the time, he sleeps. When he stirs, I try to remind us both that no dog in his right mind would want to live rough again – sleeping on wet moss and going to bed hungry – when a sofa and a variety of medically recommended 'treats' are available. Certainly not me. In my garden, I still chase small furry animals and the wind, but only for sport. I have come a long way since the people at the rescue home came to see The Man to make sure that he knew how to look after me. Meeting for the first time the dog I have become, you would never guess that I was an orphan and a foundling.

When my brother and I were only a few days old, my mother was bitten by a rat, and the builder who owned her tied her to a fencepost and left her to die. She fed us as much as she could during her dying days and then we survived on water from a leaky hosepipe. The lady who lived next door tried to rescue us, but – being young, frightened and stupid – we ran away. For months we lived on what we could scavenge from waste bins and black bags – still objects of fascination I cannot pass without a wishful sniff in memory of my scavenger days.

Then Doris caught me. She was the first person to talk to

me. I could not understand a word, but I loved the sound of the noise she made. Doris was old; in human years she was older than I am now. And since I had not even begun to put the wolf in my head to sleep, I was far too wild for her to look after for long. For more than six months I moved from one canine care home to another. At some places I lived in a cage; I hated that. At others I lived with other dogs, which – being a pack animal – I loved. But it also made me sad. Most of the other residents remained for only a couple of weeks. Then they were reunited with their owners or found a family to adopt them. But while they came and went, I stayed. I was kept warm and fed, but I had nobody who had the time to talk to me. And, thanks to Doris, talking was essential to my happiness.

When I was wild, I looked tremendous. My father was an Alsatian and my mother a Staffordshire bull terrier. The result of that irregular union combined both parents' characteristics – the lean shape of a small Alsatian and the thick brindle coat of a Staffordshire bull terrier.

Perhaps my brother never lost his good looks. But after a few months in the canine care homes, I went into a decline. My ribs showed through my skin and fur fell out of my coat. People who saw my picture thought I must be ill. And nobody chooses to adopt a sick dog. Some visitors to the canine care home imagined that I would grow up to be a fighting dog or a pit bull terrier. The Dangerous Dogs Act had just been passed by Parliament – not, it must be said, with any real opposition from The Man. Respectable people thought I might be illegal, so the only people who wanted to own me were undesirables. But I wanted friends with whom I could have the sort of conversations I had had with Doris and her friends. When a skinhead came into the canine care home, I tried to look like a Pekinese. Painful though it was to deny my heritage, I did not want to grow up wearing a collar studded with nails.

Did you know that thousands of families get dogs as Christmas presents and then abandon them in the New Year? It is hard to believe, but it is true. And the canine care homes have to make room for the outcasts and rejects in the only possible way they can. As the season of good will approached, I sat behind my wire grille and worried. Was it possible? Surely a nation of dog lovers would not allow such a thing to happen? Hearing that I was to be advertised on the Hard to Home Register only increased my apprehension. It sounded too much like the last chance of a reprieve. Then She came along, looked at me and said, 'He looks like exactly the right kind of dog for a Yorkshireman.'

My old name was something I can't recall, but The Man said it made me sound like a hairdresser who is engaged to a Second Division footballer. I think that he is a bit of a snob. But then, so am I. That is one of the many qualities we have in common.

The Man said that I have an optimistic walk, cheerful ears and that my bottom sways with self-confidence. I prefer to be described as 'swaggering' rather than 'swaying'. Whichever word you prefer, it conveys the right idea. That is why The Man decided that I should be called Buster.

And the rest is history.

At least, the first few years are. When I tried to tell the story of my early years, The Man tried to take all of the credit. You do not need me to remind you that I bravely defended myself against the Queen's kamikaze goose in St James's Park. And you will recall how I stood by The Man during the shame of his subsequent prosecution and eventual conviction for being out of control. Remember, I was never off the lead. He was. But I knew that he deserved a second chance.

To hear him tell the story of what happened after the court case, you would think that I have been 'spoilt rotten', as they say 'up North', where The Man comes from. Not so. There have been moments of callous neglect. After my celebrity guest appearance at the annual Staffordshire Bull Terrier Rescue Walk in the Lake District, he had to admit that he had forgotten my breakfast. I had to make do with the cheap dog food that was on offer at the hotel. There was even the suggestion that I would have to survive on breakfast cereal. And, because of his negligence, I had only just escaped from the jaws of death, disguised as the gap between the platform of St Pancras Station and the footboard of the 10.40 from Chesterfield to London.

I have made my way in the world by instinct and my steadfast belief in the pursuit of territory and a higher pack order. And I look forward to making more progress for some years to come. How many I cannot say. According to The Man, calculating my age in human terms, last year I was seventy. Now I am almost seventy-seven. I am not sure how old I will be next year, but I expect that I will still be healthy.

According to The Man, mongrels (I prefer to be called a cross-breed) live longer than pedigree dogs. Magnus (the dog his mother killed by giving him rich food) was a pure-bred Yorkshire terrier. And he was only nine (dog) years old when he died. After the funeral The Man's mother said that she 'could not go through it again' and would not have another dog. I still do not know what she had gone through. It was Magnus who died. The Man says he understands how she felt, and blows his nose a lot when people talk about 'losing' their dogs. I have never been lost – though, for some strange reason, The Man seems to think I will be one day. It is when this subject is mentioned that he blows his nose most loudly.

By the time I met The Man's mother, she was very old – probably fourteen or fifteen in dog years. She had had lots of dogs, all of them – she kept telling me – intelligent, loyal and well behaved. But none compared with Sally, the ugliest bitch I have ever seen. So much for the intelligent, loyal, well-behaved Magnus. When I last saw The Man's mother, she was sitting in a big armchair with two cushions behind her and Sally on the cushions, like Long John Silver and his parrot. But now The Man's mother is with Magnus, Mick, Joey, Bess and Dinah. Sally has gone to live on a farm, where she sits on the lady's lap and dominates all the other dogs.

Sally, The Man's mother and the canine care home are all behind me. They were the subjects of the stories of my youth, told in the language of my youth – and interpreted (sometimes wrongly) by The Man. The time has come to set out my own version of events – free from the obsessive who talks about me having a life of my own, but, when I am out of his sight (perhaps only stretched out on the window seat to bask in the sun and have a little sleep), shouts, 'Where's Buster?' When I go into the garden on my own, I have adventures – and he knows nothing about them. They are the most interesting part of my life.

The time has come to describe what happened to this hairy Odysseus when he reached maturity. In one sense, the second volume of diaries complements the first. It too is the story of how a dog of character can rise above his humble beginnings and it contains descriptions of the rewards that success brings. But this time I reveal the jealousies that the successful have to bear with courage and fortitude.

How often I have heard a passer-by say, 'Hello, Buster,' and then stop The Man and ask, 'Weren't you once a politician?' or tell him, 'I recognise the dog and I know I've seen you on television, but I can't remember your name.' The look of agony such approaches provoke would cause anguish in hearts that are softer than mine. I was with him in the shop in Buxton when the lady behind the counter told him, 'We've always enjoyed you in *Antiques Roadshow*.' I will never forget his tortured attempt to smile.

I am not yet ready to accept a similar obscurity. Now the time has come for the real me to emerge. No more Mr Nice Dog. This time, I report the hard truth about living with The Man. That is why I wrote my diaries in secret.

Since one of my years is equivalent to seven of the human calendar, it is sometimes hard to keep track of time, so some of the dates may be slightly wrong. But, allowing for that, everything recounted on the following pages really happened.

London, Millennium Night and Day

The Man went out unusually late. There was all the usual fuss about 'Will he be all right?' and assurances to me that he would 'not be gone for long'. In fact, he was back within a couple of hours, rather to my annoyance, since he both woke me from a deep sleep and disturbed a dream in which the vet had pre-scribed a diet that consisted entirely of Gorgonzola cheese.

'Look,' said The Man grudgingly, 'he's been fast asleep. I doubt if he even heard the fireworks. He didn't even wake up when we came in. I could hear him snoring in the hall.' I was naturally hurt by his apparent disappointment that I had – until interrupted – enjoyed a peaceful night. But I was too drowsy to do anything except perform the usual pantomime – a quick wobble of my rear to create the impression that I was glad to see him, then back into the basket and off to sleep again.

Next morning it was all forgotten. A little later than usual we were off to Green Park – St James's being out of bounds since the blatant suicide of the royal goose.

Everywhere was deserted. No buses in Victoria Street. No tourists outside Buckingham Palace. No joggers in the park. We went to our usual spot in the glade between the trees and I was let off the lead. I was about to do my morning ablutions when the unmistakable odour of half-eaten beef burgers, stale chips and greasy chicken drumsticks wafted out of Piccadilly. I pride myself on my nasal sensitivity, but even a dog without a nose – the subject of a weak joke that is constantly repeated by The Man* – would have identified the smell of delicious meat I am not allowed to sample. Naturally enough I took off out of the top gate into the road, down towards Piccadilly Circus – stopping as I went along to pick up a burger here and a drumstick there. There was not a motor car in sight.

When The Man caught me, he looked as if he was about to suffer a heart attack. It seems that it was not the exertion of the unaccustomed run that had caused the problem: he had not noticed that there was no traffic in the road and feared that I would be squashed flat by a big red bus. He concluded that my conduct proved I could no longer be trusted. I saw the whole incident in a different light. It is clear that I can venture –

* In case you are interested, this is it:
  'I have a dog without a nose.'
  'How does it smell?'
  'Awful!'

without being tied to The Man – into what he regards as forbidden territory. The time has come to break out.

Derbyshire, 3 February 2000

I am condemned to go through life in chains.

They have decided, after much agonising, that in future I must always wear a lead in public – a short one on roads, expanding in parks and other open spaces.

It hardly seems worthwhile going for a walk.

4 February

Refused to go to the park. Stood at corner of street in defiant pose, paws splayed in a way that made it difficult to drag me in the direction The Man wanted to go without risking pulling off my head. He went home and said I must be ill.

6 February

Consultations have convinced him that I am not ill but defiant. He is going to read a book to find out how to deal with me. Pathetic.

8 February

Priding himself on being of a progressive disposition, The Man thought it necessary to give me a verbal warning of what will happen if I refuse to walk tomorrow. On the advice of the book, I will be picked up, carried a few paces and then put down with a thud.

The prospect is very disturbing. The Man will do himself an injury and I will feel responsible. Then I will have to think of a way of getting him home.

However, I am not going to yield to mild blackmail.

15 February

This morning the threat was carried out.

I walked as far as Victoria Street and then sat down. After a few moments of tugging on the lead, The Man picked me up. He then realised that he could not risk carrying me across the busy road. So he (perfidiously) led me back towards home.

As soon as we got into our street, he picked me up again and staggered along (with some difficulty) in the direction of the park. Then he did not so much put me down with a bang as drop me. I walked meekly for a few paces and then again took up my 'so far but no further' position.

He picked me up, carried me and dropped me four times

more. Each time there were brief walking interludes in between.

When we got to Buckingham Palace, there was a long queue of people waiting to go into the Royal Gallery to look at the corgis. We had to walk past them. I did not want to. So The Man did it all again. Pick up. Carry. Down with a bang. The people in the queue looked amazed. He had gone through the ritual three times before he reached the back of the queue. Then – exhausted – he returned to his old primitive habits and tried to drag me along by pulling my lead.

I put on my 'please don't beat me any more' look and refused to be pulled. After a while – mostly because of embarrassment – The Man gave up and we turned for home. The people in the Buckingham Palace queue broke out into applause. One lady said, 'Game, set and match to the dog,' whatever that may mean.

16 February

I have decided that walking in the park on the end of the expanding lead is better than not walking at all. Normal behaviour will resume tomorrow.

Derbyshire, 15 March

What, I wonder, has The Man got against cow dung?

As far as I can make out – and my sense of smell is far

superior to his – it is composed of pure protein bound together with a little masticated grass and half-digested straw. Yet I am not allowed to eat it.

There is a stern rebuke if I even wander in the direction of a tempting helping, and the slightest lick produces a tug on the lead. That is a form of punishment explicitly forbidden by the RSPCA, the Canine Defence League and the Kennel Club – though the Kennel Club's rule may only apply when a pedigree dog is on the other end of the lead.

In the spring – when calves are in the fields – dung is especially high in milk content, although its green colour and slimy texture create a different impression. This morning after The Man had failed to drag me away in time and I managed to lick a huge dollop, he told me, 'No kisses tonight.' He did not mean it.

London, 17 April

The Man took me in the car to Kent to meet a professional dog trainer who turns rescue dogs into performers for the Royal Show. The Man was very sceptical. When he saw the trainer's dogs jump through hoops and walk on tightropes, he almost went home straight away. We do not believe dogs should do tricks. But he was being paid to write about dog training, so all principle was put aside. The trainer had a natural authority, and although The Man often says that I hear but do not always listen, I was all ears. The fellow said, 'Heel,' and I found myself walking a respectful pace behind him. When we reached a traffic light, I found myself sitting without being told. I wondered if I had been hypnotised. (When The Man once tried to hypnotise me – 'Buster, you are getting sleepy' – I just fell asleep.) On the way home The Man tried to rationalise his training failures. 'Just because you like authoritarian personalities, I am not going to boss you around like that.' That all goes to show why The Man is not a dog. Far too sentimental.

Derbyshire, 14 March 2001

As any sensible man would have realised, the garden – instead of a source of continual pleasure – has become the cause of constant controversy. There is no doubt that it was bought for me. It exists to allow me the running space I was denied elsewhere after my Millennium excursion into Piccadilly. The fields of Derbyshire had long been out of bounds because of my attitude towards sheep and cows. Sheep are both silly and meek. First of all they follow me and when I turn round they run away so I want to chase them. And when I first saw a herd of cattle, instinct told me to put them in a circle and keep running round them to make sure that they stayed in the same place. They belonged to Tom, the kind young farmer who owns a herd of pure-bred Charolais. And they were pregnant. He said, 'There's no problem. They didn't drop one,' which was a strange thing to say because they were not carrying anything. However, after that, I have always had to wear a lead in the country as well as town. Paradoxically (which is a big word for a dog to use), until the journey down Piccadilly, I had been allowed limited freedom in London's Green Park.

Fortunately, next door's garden came up for sale just as it seemed my whole life would be spent on the end of a leash. The garden was for me.

I would have been perfectly happy for the garden to remain as we found it – a wilderness of overgrown rhubarb, cabbage plants that had gone to seed, straggling raspberry canes and moss-covered fruit trees. Indeed, I would have preferred it to stay as it was – a neglected orchard and kitchen garden that had become home to feral cats and a variety of small furry animals. Unfortunately, The Man had other ideas.

What would have been a hunter's paradise was subjected to the ravages of garden design. The garden was divided into a series of terraces. Fortunately, a number of bushy borders remain. But the whole thing has become subject to a series of regulations. Defecation is forbidden on what is now called the croquet lawn. Urination on the new apple trees is permitted but discouraged. Most onerous of all is the obligation to move from old garden to new through a specially constructed gap in the hedge.

The hedge, which once marked the boundary of our property, is The Man's pride and joy. It is more than six feet high and three bushes thick. When we got the new garden and he had to cut a hole in it, he was almost in tears. Then She found two old stone gateposts and the hole became a 'feature'. It is a feature that I am required to use when everybody knows it is much more fun to push through a gap in the bottom of the hedge.

Well, not quite everybody. Whenever The Man hears the twigs snapping in the bottom of the hedge and sees me emerge with leaves in my fur, he announces, 'I'll make him go the proper way if it's the last thing I do.' It will not be the last thing he does because I will never do it. I have been pushing my way through the hedge for so long that it has become a habit. The radar in my brain directs me to the spot where I have made the hole and, at least twice a day, make it bigger. That is how dogs are. I would have thought he knew that.

17 July

A piece of wire netting has been fastened across the hole in the hedge. It has been pegged into the ground with garden canes. It will take about an hour either to find a way round or batter it down. In the meantime I shall stay in the old garden in order to avoid the indignity of using the official route. It is sad that the garden of which I had such high hopes should have caused a running argument between The Man and me.

London, 21 September

I am in trouble again. Dogs like people to look the same, and when they do not, we get confused. We were in the car and The Man put down the window to talk to a neighbour. The neighbour had lost part of his arm when he was an apprentice butcher. I did not know that. All I knew was that he was not symmetrical. So I barked my head off. As the neighbour got into his chauffeur-driven car, he said that all dogs bark at him. If he still smelt of meat, his canine relationship might have been very different.

28 December

The Man is getting increasingly sensitive about old age – mine as well as his. People stop us in the street and ask how old I am (which is very rude), and one person actually enquired, 'Is this the same Buster?' When The Man said that it was indeed the famous diarist, the person added, 'He must be getting on. You're lucky to have kept him this long.' The Man seemed very upset.

The person went into the big church near where we live and The Man said, 'He's wasting his time. If there really was a God, He would make dogs live as long as humans.'

11 March 2002

Since I first came to live with The Man, he has turned funny about food. First it was veal. The Man is unhappy about how the little cows live until they are turned into steak. He does not know it but I had a veal escalope once from a black bag that was torn open next to Il Paradiso. I thought I was in paradise. One bite and it was gone. Now he eats no red meat at all. Strange though that is, I do not interfere. Why can he not be equally tolerant about my eating habits?

Sometimes he is so obsessive about what goes into my mouth that he almost kills me. When I smell chicken in the street, I have to snatch it immediately and swallow straight away, for no sooner does he see a bone in my mouth than he grabs my snout. It would be much safer to let me chew it carefully, but The Man has inherited a dangerous ignorance. His mother thought that she knew everything about dogs. She said that dogs should not eat chicken bones. So he thinks so too. Fortunately, she was wrong about another aspect of dog care. She also said that it is always dangerous to take food out of a dog's mouth. Sometimes that is true. But because The Man is my friend and chose to share his life with me, I let him take food from my mouth when he wants to. He does not eat it himself, but just throws it to where I cannot reach it. Of course, I could have his hand off if I wanted to.

If I had not become too domesticated, that is exactly what

I would do — out of pure self-preservation. For when he grabs at the bone, instinct dictates that I swallow it whole — thus risking choking myself to death. It all goes to show that a dog can be killed by kindness.

4 April

After veal, it was pork. 'Buster, do you know that pigs are smarter than most six-year-old children?' Nature made us carnivores, so I hoped that he would draw the line at bacon. Bacon has a special, literary place in my heart.

The first time we went to Dartington, I was allowed in the Great Hall. Dogs are not allowed there, but The Man said, 'No dog, no speak.' Kay, who is in charge, was so impressed by The Man's commitment to animal rights that she made him president of the festival. And I went into the Great Hall.

As usual, I was made to sit in the aisle, and She tied me to her chair leg. Normally I just go to sleep, but I kept smelling bacon. I dream about it still. When we were wild, my brother and I used to wait for bacon butties to be dropped. Sometimes we did not wait; we just snatched them from children walking on Paddington Rec.

In the Great Hall, I waited until the lights went down and quietly put my snout in the bag of the lady in the seat in front. I was certain that this was where the bacon sandwich had been hidden. And so it was. The bread was warm and it was buttered with real butter. (At home, when I lick the knives in the dishwasher, all I get is what The Man's mother called 'grease'. It is supposed to be better for The Man's health, but I wonder if he knows that butter tastes much nicer.) I was licking the last of the taste from my whiskers when the lady in front reached into her bag. She made rustling noises for several minutes. Then she turned out all the contents of her bag on to her lap. The people sitting near-by turned and stared at her in disapproval. One even asked her to be quiet. On the way out, I heard her say, 'I was sure it was there when I left home.' Fortunately, she had not noticed the wrapping paper on the floor.

21 May

Full of the joys of spring. And my head has been turned. I have formed an attachment for an older bitch – and her mother.

When we go to Vincent Square, I see two sleek Hungarian vizslas. They are allowed to run around the square without a lead. They are much taller than I am, so I pull myself to my full height, hold in my stomach and prick my ears to look my best.

The Man is not very good with names. He calls them Ava and Zsa Zsa. They are really called Daisy and Flora, but they are still pedigrees and they know it.

5 June

The name thing is getting worse as a result of The Man's amusement at the idea that the Hungarian vizslas are called Ava and Zsa Zsa. He did not call me Buster once today. While I prefer Buster to the name I had in the canine care home, I am also expected to answer to Buzzy, Buzz, the Buzz and Alphonse. Alphonse is the worst. The Man says that when the Duchess of Argyll was told, 'The dog cannot go there,' she replied, 'He's not the dog – his name is Alphonse.' Now whenever anyone refers to me as 'the dog', he says, 'He's not the dog – his name is Alphonse.' Then he laughs. I do not find this funny.

Derbyshire, 24 July

Humans seem not to mind having more than one name. One of the people with two names was staying with us in Derbyshire. This one was called Roy or Lord Jenkins. Dogs get very confused when they are called by a different name. But Roy or Lord Jenkins seemed very composed. At least he was until halfway through his breakfast. He and The Man were having what humans call an 'animated discussion' about books. The Man was looking at a little yellow book with strange writing and my photo on the back – which was the front.

Roy or Lord Jenkins asked what The Man had in his hand and was told, 'It's *Buster's Diaries* in Japanese.'

The Man then asked, smiling ridiculously, 'Has your *Churchill* been translated into Japanese?'

'Ah … not yet.'

Dame Jennifer or Lady Jenkins roared with laughter. The discussion continued and became so animated that Roy or Lord Jenkins emphasised his point by waving a piece of toast.

There was no need for The Man to make such a fuss. Roy or Lord Jenkins did not even know where the piece of toast had gone. I was up from under the table (between his legs to be exact) and back again on the floor with the speed of brindle light.

The Man grabbed me by my collar and put me out into the hall. However, the humiliation was well worth it, for my daring had created an impression, which had, for me, the most significant results. And I ate the toast.

Later that day, Roy or Lord Jenkins gave a talk about Winston Churchill, the great prime minister who was often compared to a bulldog. It was one of those days when, because there is nobody in the house to look after me, I am required to attend some boring lecture and sit quietly in the audience until the applause, when I am allowed to bark. At the end of the talk, a man in the audience asked the question, how could Roy or Lord Jenkins – apparently a man of sensitivity and taste – admire Winston Churchill, who was neither of those things? Although my hearing is so well tuned that I can recognise the rustling of a crisp packet from a

hundred yards, when Roy or Lord Jenkins replied I could barely believe the evidence of my own ears.

'Let us put it like this,' he said, 'Churchill was arrogant, self-centred, aggressive and inclined to impose himself on those around him. But he was bursting with energy and charm, unquestionably optimistic and full of life – rather like Roy Hattersley's dog, Buster.' I felt so proud that I almost forgot to bark with the applause that followed.

Sheffield, 9 September

I fear the worst. The Man is turning into his mother. Today he announced that not only would he never eat meat again, but that he would boycott birds caught for sport, fish caught by rod and line, and crustaceans (which means they have shells) that are boiled to death. The Man's mother went peculiar and in the end only ate rabbit food. Please God may he not develop a similar mania and expect me to join in. The experiences at his mother's house ought to have taught him how it feels suddenly to be deprived of protein.

When we arrived, Sally, the ugliest bitch in the world, was already eating. She seems to eat all day. No wonder the dividing line round her middle – where The Man says Dr Frankenstein stitched a long-haired terrier to a short-haired whippet – has expanded. Sally's food was everywhere and The Man rushed around from room to room collecting it before I was even allowed to go into his mother's living room.

As always Sally demanded that I show the deference due to bitches. I know instinctively that dogs have to grovel to bitches and accept my temporary reduction in status with good grace. But this morning Sally insisted on taunting me. She had a mountain of toys hidden behind the old lady's electronic ejector chair. Sally brought out one toy at a time and dropped it at my feet. Then, in an annoying little yap, she announced, 'Mine. Mine.'

Five minutes after we arrived, I had endured all I could bear. I put my lead in my mouth and trotted over to The Man in my most endearing way, making it clear that I wanted to go home. I hoped that he would make an excuse and leave: 'My Buster is not very well. We're taking him home and will give him some soup' – or something like that. The Man ignored my pleas. All he could think about was his lunch. We both could smell chicken.

Lunch started with a cheese-and-onion quiche, which, when his mother went out of the room, The Man said would go directly to his feet. He added that he was glad that he had saved some room for the chicken. But then a sherry trifle arrived. The Man looked very miserable.

After lunch he found his mother carving the chicken with Sally (salivating) in attendance. The Man told her, 'I didn't think you cooked chicken.'

As usual the old lady flattened him: 'My dog must not suffer for my principles. Sally needs chicken skin to keep her coat healthy.'

The Man stuck to unhealthy prejudices, which he calls principles. 'Well, don't give any to Buster.'

26 December

I am beginning to fear that She is unfaithful. She was out all day, which is a strange thing for Boxing Day. What is more, she spent a lot of time worrying about her clothes before she left. The Man – who is only complacent – actually helped her put on a tie. She was out all day, and when she got back, my worst fears were confirmed. She smelt of other dogs. In fact, she smelt of several.

London, 8 January 2003

I got a nasty shock today.

The Man went into the dining room with a box that I think must have been a Christmas present. It was labelled 'Executive Toy. Not Suitable for Children'. It did not say, although it should have done, 'Not Suitable for Dogs'.

I naturally went in after him – 'swaggered in', as it was later described – only to be confronted with a hideous apparition. A creature, more or less in the shape of a man but no more than ten inches high, was making its way towards me – although its legs did not move. At the same time, it gave out a strange ticking sound and what passed for a head (attached to the body without the intervention of a neck) turned slow-

ly from side to side. Occasionally a single eye flashed red and green.

I fled.

At first my fright caused The Man much amusement. Then he put on his concerned face, scratched behind my ears and said that he was sorry if I had been frightened. 'Honestly, Buster, it's nothing to be afraid of. Just a bit of clockwork.' He held the hideous object towards me, and, since it had stopped rustling, I gave it a sniff. I think it was harmless. What sort of friend goes to the trouble to wind up some clockwork robot just to frighten the dog? If he sees it coming my way again, I hope that he will behave like a real friend and tread on it.

Somewhere in Cheshire, 17 February

A particularly difficult day. Months ago The Man agreed to speak at a political meeting. Now he does not want to do this and is, in consequence, very bad-tempered. Worse still, we cannot find the village in which the meeting is to be held. She is a rotten map-reader and The Man just sits behind the wheel shouting, 'I'm driving, I can't do both jobs.'

That means we have to stop again and again and ask the way. The procedure never varies. I sit on the back seat, fastened to the safety belt with the red braces that came in the box labelled 'Precious Cargo – keep your dog safe and secure throughout the journey'. As always I had bundled my rug to one side and tipped my 'unspillable' bowl on to the car floor

– filling various pairs of shoes with water and soaking a selection of motoring maps. Indeed, the whole journey took its usual course. When She wound down the window to ask directions, I barked so loudly that She could not hear the response to her enquiry. That does not matter. Because of my barking, The Man who was asked for help has not heard the question.

That is when things turn nasty. First of all there is a lot of shouting: 'My word!' and 'Buster, be quiet.' Of course, I take no notice. So The Man turns round and tries to hold my jaws closed, but he cannot reach me because he is wearing the human equivalent of Precious Cargo. Then he frees himself – something I am never allowed to do – and grabs me by the muzzle. A less reasonable dog would bite him. I just struggle, but by the time this pantomime has ended, the person from whom we were asking directions has lost patience and walked away.

We got to the meeting, but we were very late.

10 March

Signs of old age grow increasingly obvious – in The Man, but not in me. This morning we had another example of how I have weathered the years far better than he. It is, I fear, becoming a daily feature of our morning walk and a clear indication that I have escaped the senile dementia from which he is clearly suffering.

The walk begins with a biscuit – for me, not for him. The Man calls it my 'going-away present'. On my return I get a 'welcome-home gift'. Putting biscuits in his pocket is the last thing we do before we leave. We then walk three yards to the door. By the time we get there he has forgotten which pocket they are in.

A long search ensues. Handkerchiefs are pulled out. Keys are transferred from trouser to jacket. The mobile is dropped on the floor. Pens are held in his teeth. In the end, he finds the biscuits in the pocket he searched first.

And while all this is going on, my steely gaze never wanders from his searching hand. My powers of concentration are just as great as they were eleven years ago, and my stare is just as unswerving. I look at The Man and think how awful it must be to decline with age.

London, 20 March

This morning, as we left home for our walk, the road was no different from any other Sunday – dozens of cars stealing our parking places whilst their drivers and passengers pray in the cathedral for everybody to be nice to each other. When we got back, there were lorries parked in the middle of the road.

Lorries generally have people only inside the cab. But the lorries in our road had people all over them – mostly dressed in funny green clothes. Some had big plastic ears fastened to their heads with elastic. Some wore pointed hats. A giant harp

– not real, but made out of cardboard – was being hauled on to the lorry at the front of the line. 'Begorrah,' said The Man (which for some reason he thought very funny), 'my car is blocked in.'

A fat policeman was standing at the corner of our road. I thought that he was drinking something brown out of a plastic cup, but The Man said that was impossible as the policeman was on duty. The Man and I also disagree about what followed.

Both of us accept that The Man asked if it was possible to move his car. When we got back home, I was assured that the fat policeman had only used his mobile telephone to point to the far end of the road and had put his arm round The Man's shoulder as a gesture of friendship. From where I observed the scene, only eighteen inches above the pavement, it looked different. To me, it seemed that the fat policeman had The Man's neck in an armlock and was about to strike him with a blunt, heavy instrument. In consequence I did my duty.

Even when The Man shouted, 'My God,' I did not realise that I had made a terrible mistake. Looking back, I naturally feel glad that I did nothing more than tear open the policeman's shirt from top to bottom. But I still think that my only crime was an excess of zeal. Fortunately, the policeman agreed.

After the first 'My God', The Man seemed unable to speak, but the fat policeman spoke a lot and very quickly. I could not understand what he was saying, for he spoke with a strange accent, which The Man said was Irish. He also must have come from a place called Slur, for The Man also said his speech was slurred. After he had stopped jumping about and looking at his exposed stomach, he admitted what I had known to be true from the beginning. 'The dog did right. It was my fault. I should not have put my hand on you.'

The Man was still speechless, but when the fat policeman said, 'If he'd done it to a member of the general public, I would have had to report you,' The Man gradually came back to life and said, 'Do you mean…?'

'Take him home,' said the fat policeman. 'Take him home quick.'

The Man was about to take the fat policeman's advice when a lady, dressed in a long, black dress with a black hood over her head, came up to us and looked at the fat policeman's stomach. 'The skin's broken,' she said. 'Shall I drive you to hospital?'

It was clear to me that The Man had not regained his composure, for he called the lady 'sister' and I happen to know he was an only child. 'Sister,' he said, 'for heaven's sake, we are in enough trouble as it is.'

I do not know what trouble we were in. I had done my duty and received a police commendation. But The Man seemed to be in a stupor for the rest of the morning. When we got home, he just sat in a chair and stared into space.

Derbyshire, 25 March

A bird got into our sitting room. We didn't know if it came down the chimney or flew in the front door when nobody was looking. I am usually looking. But I could have been asleep on the half-landing. I sleep more and more these days.

The Man's attempts to catch it were pathetic. I could have dealt with it in a couple of minutes. But I was locked out of the room while he blundered about. Even when he caught it, he only put it out in the garden instead of killing it.

London, 13 April

I am thinking of suing the Post Office. This morning, the postlady, instead of pushing the envelopes through the letter-box, left a bundle of letters outside the front door. I shall not sue them for leaving the letters lying about. They do that all the time. The cause of my complaint is a card that I found in the bundle. It was a garish orange colour and was headed 'Special Instruction'. There followed a variety of meaningless numbers – 'P395', 'op/01266 11/87' and 'Rev'd Mar 27'. Then, below the crudely written heading 'Information', an extraordinary message had been written inside the box marked 'Special Instructions': 'The Dog can be Dangerous. Please take care of yourself and be vigilant. Harold Peterson, MANAGER.'

That is a clear libel. I am not dangerous. Nor is there any evidence to suggest otherwise. I am boisterous. When I leap at postpersons and others, my only intention is to show friendship. Thanks to the Post Office, the old letter controversy has reared its ugly head.

15 April

It seems the postperson claims that as she approaches, I leap at the letterbox. This is not true. I never leap at the letterbox. I leap at the letters. Neither She nor The Man seemed reassured by the reassurance that my only interest is the envelopes. For some reason that I find incomprehensible, they do not want their letters to be perforated by teeth marks. I cannot see much ground for compromise.

22 April

More trouble with transport. The Man seems incapable of realising that I will never be reconciled to crash helmets. The best that he can do is to switch into his 'do-it-yourself Freudian-analysis' mode and speculate about the possibility of me having been badly treated, in youth, by a male motorcyclist.

The simple fact is that I do not like human beings who are the wrong shape. Men are supposed to have hair or skin on top. Women just have hair. I like people to be natural. If God had meant men to have steel where their scalps should be, He would have made them all like that – not just motorcyclists, who cruise up to the side of our car and stare in at me through the window. My barking is supposed to indicate determination to repel boarders.

2 May

We have been asked to leave the premises of Wellington Hall, a university hall of residence near Vincent Square, where I sometimes walk. We were there because of a medical emergency, but the person who asked us to leave could not be made to understand. He was not English. When The Man said, 'Not out. In,' and tried to explain our problem with gestures, the foreign person seemed to be offended. Our intentions were clear enough.

I now rely on alternative medicine – sometimes known as grass. No other treatment has the same, almost instant, effect on my most frequent indisposition. I suffer from chronic sickness – usually brought on by eating refuse. The Wellington Hall garden is the nearest grass to where we live.

My preventative medicine comes from the vet – at great expense, as The Man never tires of telling me. But at moments when my stomach is in turmoil, only grass will do.

Fortunately, I can usually tell when a bad turn is coming on. I signal the imminent crisis by rushing from room to room looking for grass. We never have any in the house. So

The Man, recognising my needs, takes me where it can be found. Then, in his words, I 'eat enough to stuff a cushion'. The result is always immediate. I am violently sick and feel ready for anything – including eating refuse.

The Man says that belief in what he calls 'herbal remedies' makes me a freak. It also makes me healthy. If he ate grass he would be able to walk faster. And he would not have been afraid of the foreign person who turned us out of the Wellington Hall garden.

Aboard a Train on the Route of the Flying Scotsman, 4 May

We travelled on the train for hours. The Man could not wait until lunch and started to eat his sandwiches as soon as the train left Chesterfield. I had to be tied to the table leg by the bright-red Precious Cargo safety belt that I wear in the motor car. And my jaws were held together by a device called a 'halty'. I was able to eat, drink and breathe, but I could not communicate or show my clean, shiny teeth. As a result, it did not seem worth barking.

Every hour or so The Man feigned concern and said, 'Poor Buster. We must drive to Edinburgh next year.' We used to drive, but The Man was photographed by a camera hidden behind a bush in the Borders. He swore and mumbled something about three points. I happen to know that he could have had another nine points before being banned. He chose the train so he can eat and drink during the journey. However, he felt guilty about the drinking and took off my muzzle to offer me some water so often that I found it difficult to settle into steady sleep.

Fortunately, he remembered my red plastic travelling bowl with spill-proof lid – for once. When he forgot my bowl last week, I had to drink out of a glass. The Man always says, 'Buster does not do tricks.' But when I drank from a glass, he shouted, 'Well done, Buster. You are clever.' He hoped that the other passengers would be impressed by the way I had been trained.

I got to sleep by York, but The Man woke me for what he called a 'pit stop'. We raced along the compartment and leapt out on to the platform. It is not easy to perform to order. But when the guard blew his whistle, I cocked my leg against a packing case that was waiting to be put on the train. Begrudging as always, The Man said, 'Better there than nowhere.'

Derbyshire, 14 June

They were having supper in the yard – 'al fresco', The Man said. The yard is the nearest he gets to Tuscany since I became his friend. I was in my regulation place under the table waiting for crumbs to bounce off The Man's stomach or fall from his lap. Imagine my surprise when a cat dropped from the wall into my yard. I am excessively territorial, but even if I were a placid sort of a chap, such an invasion would be a *casus belli.*

The cat was ancient – over twenty. So even if I had only looked, it would have died of fright. However, I caught it by the back of the neck and gave it a good shake. It felt nothing, but The Man was terribly upset and locked me in the kitchen while he went round to all the neighbours to see if anyone was missing a cat. She rang a vet to find out how She could make sure that its nine lives were up.

After several hours of anxiety, The Man decided to bury the cat in the garden. It is the first gardening he has done for himself since we moved to Derbyshire.

15 August

A lady from up the road came round with photos of her cat. She had been on holiday. The Man thought the cat was a kitten because it was so thin. But it was so thin because it was so old. 'All I want to know,' she said, 'is if it is dead. It was very old and I feared it had crawled away to die.' You see, I did it a favour.

When the lady asked, 'Are you sure it's mine?' The Man said, 'Yes. Yes,' very quickly. 'That's certainly the one.' He was clearly afraid that he would have to dig it up for identification.

London, 3 September

There is a magic fox in Vincent Square. We see it every night we are in London when we go for our last walk of the day.

The magic fox lives inside the railings on Westminster School's playing fields. When we walk round outside the railings, it walks with us – sometimes running ahead and sometimes loitering behind and then catching us up.

The Man is very afraid that the magic fox will attack us. It disappears from time to time, as we walk round the square, and then reappears a few seconds later. It is, however, magic for quite a different reason.

The bars on the Vincent Square railings are about three inches apart. The magic fox is at least twice as broad. But when it wants to, it can make itself thin enough to skip through the railings and back again. If it did bite me, perhaps I could have the magic too.

3 October

I have been to church.

The Man went last night to give a talk in a place called Epworth. John Wesley used to live there. The Man wrote a book about him. He thought that the talk was in the church hall, but he was wrong. It was in the church. At first we were not sure what to do. But The Vicar, the name of the person in charge, said, 'Bring Buster in.' The Man said that The Vicar must be an admirer of St Francis. Is he the big hairy one with the brandy cask round his neck who rescues people from the snow?

Derbyshire, 20 October

I think The Man has gone crazy. Before I am allowed out into the garden, he makes a preliminary reconnoitre to make sure that there are no cats in the bushes. He is particularly concerned about a ginger tom that makes regular visits to stalk birds. The Man thinks that Ginger is too fat to escape me.

25 October

I am very wet.

The ginger cat who comes into my garden was back this evening. I caught sight of it in the bushes, but too late. It dashed through the orchard and climbed the silver birch tree near to the old horse trough that has fish in it.

I thought that there was a lid on the horse trough, for I could see that something was holding up a lot of leaves that had fallen from the trees. So I jumped on to the lid to get three feet nearer to the cat in the tree.

The leaves were held up by a piece of wire netting, which was there to keep them out of the water. It did not keep me out of the water.

And the cat got away.

Cheltenham, 20 November

I woke up in an hotel. Instead of smelling of me, my bed smelt of something very clean. I was not sure where I was, but I could hear The Man snoring so I went to his bed and gave him a scratch. Instead of saying, 'Back to bed, Buster,' he said, 'Buster looks nervous. He needs a cuddle.' He sat on the side of his bed and let me put my feet on his knees and we rubbed heads together. Feeling better, I went back to bed. It turned out to be something called a counterpane, which had been folded up and put on the floor for my exclusive use. This accounted for the strange smell. Later, I heard The Man say, 'He was back asleep within seconds, but I couldn't get off again.' That made no sense. He got off the bed almost straight away.

London, 12 December

Another shaming example of The Man's attempts to become a dog. With him, imitation, although flattering, is the cause of constant embarrassment.

Sometimes, when we are out walking in London, he says, 'Must get money, Buster,' and we go to what he calls a bank and he stands very close to the wall. I often stand very close to walls. But when The Man does it, he keeps both feet on the ground. I lift one leg and rest it against the wall.

This morning, while standing against the wall, The Man needed to blow his nose. So, when he got his handkerchief out of his pocket, he tried to hold his wallet in his mouth. Any toothless old retriever could have done it without difficulty. But The Man spluttered and dropped it in the road, scattering ten-pound notes on the pavement.

These days he finds it difficult enough to bend down to pick up after me. The sight of him trying to retrieve the banknotes before they blew away is not something I want to witness again.

5 January 2004

Much rejoicing. The Man has been asked to appear on a 'celebrity' television show. His pleasure is only slightly spoilt by discovering he is not to be one of the celebrities. 'Never mind, Buster,' The Man said, as if I cared, 'it's all for charity.'

The show is based on a regular series called *They Think It's All Over*. The Man is to appear in front of a panel of blindfolded real celebrities who have to guess who he is. They try to find out by touching him all over. A panel of dogs would give a sniff at his trouser leg and identify him at once.

9 January

More rejoicing. This time by me. I am to go on the television programme with The Man. This will make him easy to identify. He will wear ermine robes (to prove he is a peer) and a cloth cap (to pretend he is still a worker) and carry a tub of lard (to remind viewers of the time when he did not turn up for *Have I Got News for You?* and the lard took his place – and won). He is to hold me on the end of a short lead. David Gower is on the panel of celebrities. As well as appearing on television, I shall be stroked by an English cricket captain.

13 January

A black day indeed. I am to be excluded from the television show. The BBC, who have vetoed my appearance, have blamed their insurance company, the Health and Safety Executive and the RSPCA for their decision. The Man and I believe that one of the panel is frightened of dogs.

The Man will still appear on the television show, although there are principles at stake. It is the duty of a public broadcasting corporation neither to yield to pressure from authority nor to disappoint me. The Man ought to strike in sympathy. But although he is always so keen for me to learn new words, he does not know the meaning of solidarity.

24 January

The Man left for the BBC with the borrowed ermine robes in a carrier bag. She went with him. Although She usually refuses even to pick up parcels, She carried a big brown-paper parcel with the word 'Hattersley' printed on the outside. It smelt of sawdust.

When they got back, he came in first and shut me in the kitchen. This was strange. I usually only get shut in the kitchen when the postman or another intruder comes to the door. After a lot of rustling in the hall, I was let out. A large imitation dog, with a Hamleys label hanging round its neck, sat by the door. I think it was supposed to be a husky.

She and The Man stood there waiting for something dramatic to happen. Had I been in a better mood, I would have put on an act for them – attacking the fake husky and fastening my jaws in the back of its neck or pretending to believe it was a bitch and attempting to make passionate love. But I did neither because I was deeply offended. The lifeless creature had taken my place on the celebrity television show. And my closest friends and supposed admirers expected me to mistake it for a real dog, so I just sat there waiting to receive the biscuit that I am always given when The Man returns home. It was the thing in the hall, not me, that was the dummy.

Derbyshire, 27 January

My suspicions have been confirmed. The situation is worse than I feared.

This morning it all happened again. The Man tied her tie and She went off – not in the car but in a big lorry.

At about noon The Man asked me if I wanted to see her –

a strange question since I see her every day – and then took me out on to the village green. There were a lot of people there already, looking down the road. When we arrived, they all ignored The Man and said, 'Hello, Buster.'

One of the people said, 'There they are – I can see them.' I could see nothing except legs and feet. That did not put me at much of a disadvantage because, unlike the humans, I could smell what they were looking at. The smell was horses. I don't like horses.

After a few minutes I could smell dogs as well and I could hear a sort of barking I had never heard before. Not howling. Not whining. Not yapping. It was only because I am an expert in such matters that I recognised it as dogs at all.

Then the dogs themselves appeared – dozens of them. It takes a lot to frighten me, but I admit to being absolutely terrified. It was not just the numbers. The dogs were huge – almost as big as Brendon, the Irish wolfhound. And they were all exactly the same. I began to pull in the direction of home, but The Man said, 'Wait a minute, we want to see her.' I had seen more than enough. How would he have felt to be confronted with dozens of humans, all three times as big as him and exactly the same?

Then She rode up on a big brown horse – smiling as if She had nothing to be ashamed of. She was wearing one of those crash helmets that contribute to my dislike of motorcyclists. There were a lot of other people on horses. They all wore motorcycle helmets. After hanging around pointlessly for a minute or two, The Man said we could go home. In the house, I felt brave again and I watched the strange dogs through the window.

They had huge ears that flopped about – unlike mine, which stand on end when I tell them to. And there were rolls of floppy flesh round their necks. Too many biscuits, I expect. They all wanted to stand on their hind legs with their front paws on people. When I do that, The Man always says, 'Get down, Buster.' But the people seemed to like it when the floppy-eared giants leant on them. It is called the attraction of novelty.

When She came home, The Man said, 'I don't think Buster liked your dogs' – which was an understatement.

She said, 'They're not dogs, they're hounds. Eighteen and a half couples of bloodhounds.'

If they come round here again, I am staying inside. They are not going to hound my blood.

London, 1 February

The Man got all sentimental this morning. It happened in Vincent Square, where I go on my morning walk to cock my leg on the hole in the fence behind which Bensen, the boxer, lives. His man is in charge of the playing field in Vincent Square. There are signs everywhere, which The Man reads aloud: 'Strictly No Dogs'. Only Bensen is allowed to run on Vincent Square cricket and football pitch – and small boys in smart uniforms. But most of the time Bensen is confined to the yard behind the slatted wooden fence. When I pass and leave my scent, he barks fiercely and crashes into the rails. He is right to defend his territory – of course I know that, but I like to wind him up with a cheery, scented greeting.

Once, I was allowed in Vincent Square to have my photograph taken for the *Daily Mail*. I had always wanted to go inside, but my day was so hot that I spent the whole time panting. I know that The Man likes me to be photographed looking like my Alsatian father. He waves biscuits at me and shouts, 'Pocket, pocket,' until I sit with my ears pricked and my mouth closed. When I smell biscuits, my mouth just falls open. And when it is hot, my air-conditioning system requires me to open my mouth and show all my lovely teeth like my Staffordshire bull terrier mother. The Man does not like teeth – only cleaning them. When we wrestle – a rather boring business that I take part in to indulge The Man – he shouts, 'No teeth. No teeth. No one likes teeth except Buster.' I like teeth very much. Panting in the heat, I thought I looked like the wolf that lives inside me – all wild and menacing. The Man said that my mouth opens as far back as my eyes.

I used to go to Vincent Square before Bensen was born. The Man says that, like the Irish wolfhounds who live in Derbyshire, boxers do not live long. Before Bensen, there was another boxer called Jake, who looked just like him. The Man always gets Bensen's name wrong and calls him Jake. Then he remembers that Jake is dead. Today he said, 'Jake can't have been much older than you, Buster.' That is when he went all sentimental.

14 February

I have a pain in my face. Because I cannot eat on one side of my mouth, biscuits spill out on to the floor. Everybody is too stupid to realise that I have a problem. All they do is tell me to lick up the crumbs. Tragic. After all our years of friendship, The Man and I still have a communication problem.

19 February

I refused to have the right-hand side of my teeth cleaned tonight. Surely The Man has got the message now.

20 February

This morning, even before I had breakfast, The Man set one chair in the corner of the kitchen and asked me to put my front paws on his knees as if I was going to have my teeth cleaned. Then he pulled up the lip on the right side of my face – a privilege granted to few – and stared into my mouth. 'I'm afraid so,' he said to She. 'One's all black and broken.' Then he spoke to me. 'It's the vet for you tomorrow.' He then said a very stupid thing. 'All that tooth-brushing has not worked.' Of course it has worked. It always sends me to bed with a nice taste in my mouth.

21 February

The vet is not a vet any more. He is a partner in a Small Animal Welfare Centre and Medical Clinic – a far too important job to allow him time to worry about one black and broken tooth. So I saw a young assistant, who was kind but cautious. He would not put his fingers anywhere near my teeth, but asked The Man to hold my mouth open while he stared into it from a safe distance. He did kneel on the floor, however, instead of putting me on the table. That is clearly the new technique and one I much prefer.

Even on the floor, I hate what I still call the vet's. It was here that I had my mystery operation when I was young. Nobody would tell me what it was for. And, since I did not seem to have anything wrong with me, I cannot understand why it was necessary. I remember how unhappy it made The Man. And I recall his mother – the owner of Sally, the ugliest bitch in the world – saying, 'Oh, no! Don't tell me you've had that done to him. It's unnatural.'

The Man said that he did not like it either but it was unavoidable. What annoys me is not that it was unnatural or unavoidable but that it is still unmentionable.

The nice vet who got down on the floor said that I must have a tooth out. I know that I had something removed all those years ago. I wonder if that was a tooth as well.

2 March

Whenever we go to the vet, the procedure is always the same. We get up early in the morning. I am not allowed breakfast. Then we drive off after She has told The Man, 'Don't be silly. He'll never know it has happened.'

When we get to the vet's, we sit in the waiting room for a long time. That is a strain on both The Man and me. There are a lot of cats in baskets and birds in cages. Once, there was a lady with a rabbit in a box.

As usual, after a long wait, a lady came and led me away to have the needle stuck in me. I went to sleep at once. It seemed a long time between waking up and The Man coming to get me. When he arrived, he pulled up my lip and looked into my mouth. Then he said, 'Come on, Old Gap Tooth. Let's go home.' Why does he call me Old Gap Tooth? He knows my name is Buster.

Derbyshire, 23 March

The Man found me standing in the utility room. I had been there for a long time. He asked if I had forgotten why I went in there. I had. These days I often stand in the hall or kitchen with no clear idea why I went there. I knew from his tone that he was mocking me. Dogs, especially proud dogs like me, do not like to be mocked. So I quickly went to my water bowl and had a drink. 'Nice recovery, Buzz,' said The Man. But I had not recovered.

2 April

There has been an incident while we were walking. I was certainly not to blame. I cannot say the same about The Man.

I can't keep count of the number of dogs in our village. But as well as Angus – who lives next door and collects dead birds after his owner shoots them – there are at least a dozen, whom I recognise by their smell.

Bracken, the Irish wolfhound who I thought was the biggest dog in the world, disappeared, but came back a couple of weeks later much smaller and called Brendon. After about a year, he grew back to his original size and became Brendon Bracken. (The Man was clearly very pleased with himself for thinking of this. I cannot imagine why.) Then The Man said, mysteriously, 'Eight years isn't bad for a dog of that sort.'

At the other end of our part of the village, there is a black Labrador bitch called Molly who is said to like a good fight. She does not like me and I keep out of her way. So do most of the dogs in the village. Nearby, there is an admirable and very well-trained sheepdog who lives with Mr Poulter who is a big noise in the Mountain Rescue team. The Man's friend Professor Geoffrey Smith – who used to be a heart surgeon, which is a sort of vet for humans – sometimes looks after

Charlie, his daughter's retired greyhound. It is hard to imagine Charlie sprinting round a track. His party trick is lying absolutely still – not even moving one of his long eyelashes. When The Man first saw him lying by Professor Smith's fire, he thought that Charlie was a china dog from Harrods, which, when you compare it with how quickly I recognised the Hamleys dummy, shows who is the brightest member of our pack.

But I digress. This morning, three dogs who were not previously known to me attacked me totally gratuitously. The Man must have seen them coming. He can see over the long grass when I cannot. But despite what President Bush's spaniel would have called a 'real and present danger', he still took me into one of the narrow, wall-lined cart tracks from which there is no escape.

After it was all over, he said (rather feebly, I thought), 'How was I to know?' What he meant was that the three dogs were overweight retrievers – a naturally un-aggressive breed – and they were with a middle-aged lady in a hat, an equally timid species. Unfortunately, The Man's initial assessment proved not to be correct. One of the dogs charged at me snarling and bit me on my rump. The other two moved in for the kill. The Man, ineffectually attempting to come to my rescue, tripped and fell on top of me. For a moment I feared that, having been saved from the savage jaws, I would be crushed to death. But I was only winded and The Man sustained no more than superficial injuries to his pride.

The Man's recovery was magnificent. With the savage dogs under control, he thought it safe to stand up. 'Do you realise,' he asked the middle-aged lady in a hat, 'if I had not thrown myself on top of Buster, they might have killed him?' There was the clear implication that he would have gladly sacrificed his life for me. The middle-aged lady in the hat was crying too much to speak. When we got back home, he inspected my wounds and callously pronounced them trivial. He then wrote an angry letter to the middle-aged lady in the hat. That is all very well, but in the future I hope that he will look where we are going.

London, 18 April

There has been another incident for which I should clearly not be held responsible – though I was.

Late last night She was putting the day's rubbish outside the front door when I smelt something suspicious in the entrance hall. It was my clear duty to investigate. So – ignoring the siren call of the black bag – I rushed out. Imagine my astonishment at seeing two alien Yorkshire terriers tethered to the table where the porter's cabin used to be.

It subsequently transpired that both dogs belonged to a man who had gone abroad and left them in the care of a lady who lives in a flat on a higher floor. She was outside bringing in groceries, or something, from her car. So the dogs – over which she had *locus parentis* – were left in the hall. To me, they were simply intruders and so I took the appropriate action. The necklock comes absolutely naturally to me. I clamped on to the nearest of the apparent twins. It would have been a dereliction of duty to have done anything else.

When She screamed, The Man came rushing out. But instead of helping me repel the intruders, he intervened on their behalf. First of all he tried to force my mouth open. But my Staffordshire terrier jaws were too strong for him. Then he put his hand inside my collar and twisted it until I was so short of breath that I had to relax my grip. The miscreant escaped.

The lady from upstairs, in nominal charge of the two small, rat-like dogs, came back in with her arms full of parcels. She examined my teeth marks and judged that no great harm had been done. The Man suggested they should be taken to the vet. He offered to pay, which was surprising because he is always making jokes about the great expense I incur by having private healthcare.

3 May

A message from the lady who lives upstairs and was looking after the Yorkshire terriers. The dog with the marks in its neck is going to see a vet after all, just as a precaution. The Man has agreed to pay the bill.

4 May

I am back in the newspapers. The owner of the Yorkshire terriers has returned to Britain and is quoted in the *Evening Standard* as denouncing both me and The Man. He told them that my behaviour should be covered by the Dangerous Dogs Act – even though it says nothing about the relationship between one dog and another and I am not dangerous. Then he suggests that, one day, I might sink my teeth into the back of a baby's neck. I am sure I would never do any such thing. Anyway, it seems unlikely that two babies will ever be tethered, late at night, to the table leg outside my front door, while the lady who looks after them goes out to the car for the groceries. The Man tells me not to worry. The *Evening Standard* story is the penalty of fame – my fame.

10 May

I am a prisoner in my own home. A steel gate has been hung just inside the front door. New rules have been decreed. It must only be opened when the front door is closed, and the front door has to be closed when the gate is open. I can no longer get at the letters. But the steel gate does provide further proof of dog's superiority to man. The gate does not swing open and shut. It slides along a rail on the hall floor.

Humans always trip over the rail – even when they know it is there. I have never tripped over the rail.

Derbyshire, 22 May

Today, I was subjected to the ultimate indignity – flea treatment. I do not have fleas. I have never had fleas. I scratch because I like scratching. The Man knows that, but he has brought home a packet labelled 'Blitzkrieg – eliminates fleas, ticks and lice in seconds'. And he expects me to be grateful. 'A flea collar would be much worse. Look …' he said, pointing at the picture on the explanatory leaflet with childish glee. It was a crude drawing of a soldier who, while pointing his machine gun at a giant insect, explained, 'Prevents growth of the larvae eggs and pupae for up to eight weeks. Please wash your hands after use.' When The Man said, 'We'll do it tonight,' he tried to make it sound as if he was promising me a treat.

23 May

Last night was worse than I feared. I had to have my collar removed. I feel naked without my collar. I wear it night and day, and the medallion, with The Man's name and telephone number engraved on it, gives a merry tinkle to which I have grown attached.

Then She parted the hair on the back of my neck and squirted something sticky on my skin. Fortunately, it was bedtime, and, after my teeth had been cleaned, I quickly dropped off.

When The Man put my collar back on this morning, he said – reassuringly – 'No trouble with fleas now.' He cannot get it into his head that I never have had trouble with fleas.

26 May

According to the leaflet in the Blitzkrieg packet, I am now free of infestation for three months. But The Man was bitten again in the night. Why does he never blame the mosquitoes? Sometimes I think my only purpose is to be blamed.

Then The Man sings to me and I forgive him every indignity. One of his favourites is 'Oh, Lord, Won't You Get Me a Big Buster Dog?'*

The lyrics are childish, but I like the attention when he sings to me, especially if my name appears frequently in the lyrics.

---

* Unmusical readers may like to know that the song is based on the car advertisement. The full version is:

Oh, Lord, won't you get me a big Buster dog?
My friends all have poodles, they look like a frog.
I'll take him out walking in rain, snow or fog.
Oh, Lord, won't you get me a big Buster dog?

Derbyshire, 28 May

I like to lie on the windowsill and guard the house from walkers who change into their walking boots. They must be rebuked with a battery of fierce barks. The steel gate may stop me from jumping at the door in London, but in Derbyshire the postman knows that the moment he approaches I will be down the stairs as fast as my legs will carry me to rescue the letters. And something that The Man calls 'adrenalin' pulses through my veins and enables me to leap more than twice my height to the window in the door. The Man had to put bank-vault glass in the window to keep me from hurtling through it.

Life in the country is not all go, and for long stretches I can snooze with the sun on my back. The Man did not realise until recently that when I snore with my eyes open I am asleep. He thought I was snoring while I was awake until Professor Smith explained about my secret eyelids. I like to keep some secrets from The Man, but he is determined that I have no life of my own.

18 June

There is a lump on my leg. The Man found it while I was having my nightly brushing. It does not hurt, but it does stick out. I am perfectly calm, but The Man is near to hysterics. He promises a visit to the vet as if it were something to look forward to. I hate visiting the vet. Why do vets always want to stick needles in me?

20 June

The vet says my lump must be removed. But he cannot do it today because I have had breakfast. Back – no doubt to have a needle stuck in me – the day after tomorrow.

21 June

Concern over my leg has not stopped The Man from being increasingly difficult about the garden. The trouble began when I caught what he called a vole and he had to bury it in one of the borders. Assuming that there were more where that one came from, I wanted to stand very still and stare into one of the rose bushes so that I could get the next one to venture out. Since I was silent and absolutely motionless, I caused The Man absolutely no trouble. But he kept telling me to move about, which was strange because he usually tells me to be still. Thanks to him, no more voles appeared.

22 June

As predicted, a needle has been stuck in me.
   The experience was worse than I expected. When it is the

needle for my annual booster, The Man holds me while it happens and says things like, 'It's OK, Buster, I'm here.' That does not stop the needle from pricking me, but at least it distracts my attention.

Today, I was led away by a young lady who was not a vet. But she stuck a needle in me all the same. Fortunately, I went to sleep before I had time to wonder why The Man had left me. When I woke up, there was a bandage on my leg where the lump had been.

I had to wait a long time for The Man to come and get me. I waited in a cage – which was awful as it reminded me of the worst sort of canine care home.

There was a lot of sympathetic talk on the way home, though The Man seemed in better spirits than he had been when he took me to the vet. He made a call on his mobile to tell She that 'It was benign' – whatever that means. Then he said, 'It's the only benign thing about him.' That must have been a joke because he laughed a lot, as he always does at his own jokes.

You would have thought that since I was walking wounded, there would have been no fuss over the garden for a day or two. Not a bit of it. I had barely got home when I heard him shout, 'Straight through the bloody hedge! Look what he's doing now! He's peeing on one of the apple trees.'

For once, She was on my side. 'I told you that you should have taken him up the road.'

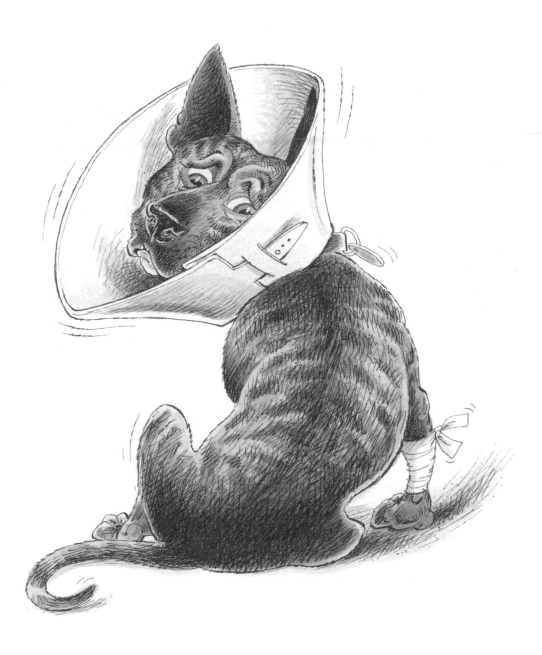

23 June

The bandage on my leg is beginning to itch. Naturally enough I scratch it, and when the scratching does not work, I attack it with my teeth. The Man says, 'Stop it, Buster,' but that is an unreasonable request which I ignore. Dogs are supposed to be able to cure themselves with spit. As a punishment he has forced me to wear a lampshade round my neck.

The lampshade is called a Buster Collar. When I first heard of it, I felt quite flattered. A collar named after me. Then I saw this strange plastic thing that stuck out round my neck and prevents me from licking any part of my person. While it remains in place, my high standard of personal hygiene will certainly deteriorate. And the bandage will go on itching. How can they do this to someone they are supposed to look after and love?

Somewhere on the M6, 6 July

Although I am a convalescent, we are all driving again to Dartington, which is a long way away. The Man is to give a talk on his latest book. With any luck I shall be put into the care of a lady called Mary Wesley. I sit with her every year. She once told The Man, 'Buster tried to get up my skirt. But I know how to deal with that. It's happened before.' He laughed – which was strange, because he usually only laughs at his own jokes and what she said did not seem very funny to me.

Two good things happened to me at Dartington. The bandage on my leg has stopped itching and the hated Buster Collar has been removed.

8 July

No sign of Mary Wesley. But even without her, I received the respect that I, as an author in my own right, am due. The lady who draws the pictures of the speakers did not draw her usual picture of The Man. Instead, she drew me, lying on my side asleep. In the picture, I am still wearing my bandage. What a good thing the hated Buster Collar had gone. It would have obscured my firm jawline and clear eyes.

Derbyshire, 14 July

A very wet day – like yesterday, the day before and the day before that. I do not like the rain, but, for reasons of personal hygiene, it is necessary for me to go out four times a day. The Man covers himself up in hat, raincoat and big boots, but I am exposed to the elements. Years ago The Man did buy me a green oilskin raincoat. But I did not like the way it fastened under my chin and round my stomach. So I scratched it off. When he got me another raincoat that only fastened under my stomach, I scratched that off too. So now I just get wet.

The good thing about getting wet is getting dry. When we get back home, The Man always takes me through the kitchen into the utility room and dries me on my own special towel. I know how special the towel is because if The Man ever looks like using it, She screams at him, 'Don't use that. It's Buster's towel.'

I like being dried. The Man rubs me all over, first down my back, then along my stomach, and, after he has dried my paws and legs, he makes sure that I am not wet under what he calls my 'armpits'. That, he says, is where dogs get pneumonia. When he says that, She always laughs.

Good though being dried is, what happens afterwards is even better. The Man always gives me a biscuit. It has rained so much this last week that I have had four extra biscuits every day.

15 July

It did not rain. So I did not get wet. But, being a creature of habit, and loving biscuits, as soon as we got home, I went into the utility room and stood next to my towel. The Man said, 'Don't be silly, Buster. There's no need to dry you.' But he still gave me a biscuit. I must be his best friend.

21 July

Much excitement during our walk this morning!

We set out to go towards the Edge, but there were so many cows about that The Man thought that we should not try to force our way through. I could have forced my way through in a second. Perhaps that is why The Man did not want me to try. Whatever the reason, we went back through the village and into the fields that lead to the Monsal Trail, which was once a railway line but is now a gentle walk.

The Man hates taking me over stiles. He is afraid of my breaking a leg and him breaking his neck. After he has helped me over, he always ties the lead to one of the stile posts before he climbs over himself. He does not want to be balancing on the top rail, holding my lead, when I see a rabbit and dash off. Were that to happen, he would not be standing on the top rail for long. As long as I am tied to the stile post, he has a chance of keeping his balance.

This morning he decided to avoid all the boring business of helping me over the stile and tying my lead to the post by cutting across the corner of a field through a gate that had been left open for cows to go through. In this part of the world, there are cows everywhere.

So many cows had gone through the open gate that the ground had been churned up into mud. I found no difficulty in picking my way over the few hard bits that stuck out of the mud. But The Man, who takes a size nine and a half, had to put his foot in it. His green wellingtons sank in to well above the ankle. Suddenly, he looked six inches shorter than usual.

I really believed that when he cried out, he wanted me to hurry on out of the mud. So, obedient as always, I leapt forward. On the other end of the lead, so did The Man. But his green wellington boots stayed where they were. When he cried, 'Wait!' with unusual authority, I turned to see him on his hands and knees in the mud. The sight caused me great distress. Humans were not meant to go through life on all fours. I went back to give him a consoling kiss. I was rejected.

Much to my regret, the walk was then abandoned. When we got home, I went (as always) into the utility room to be dried – even though I was not wet. The Man ignored me. Instead, he sat on the floor and took off his wellington boots. His socks were covered in mud. He took them off too. His feet were as muddy as his socks. I went to my bed in the kitchen and decided to clean myself. It seemed unlikely that I would be offered a biscuit for some time.

29 July

Catastrophe. Next month we are to go to Edinburgh, where I am to make my annual appearance at the Book Festival. But The Man has received a letter from the Balmoral Hotel, at which we always stay. It has been redecorated and is even more expensive than usual. But although prices have increased, dogs are no longer allowed. We will have to stay in a dump and I will be blamed every time something goes wrong. Slow room service. 'If it wasn't for Buster ...' Not enough towels. 'Whose fault is that?' As soon as I hear those words, I cannot but show my teeth and run round in a circle. She says that I am showing guilt. The Man foolishly thinks that I cannot understand guilt and that I am just being craven in the face of disapproval.

30 July

Believe it or not, The Man has had a brilliant idea. He suggested that I write a letter to the Balmoral Hotel. It began, 'Is it true that you will not have me to stay any more?' I went on to say that I had stayed there so often that it was a second home to me.

2 August

The Balmoral Hotel has replied. Apart from fan mail and proposals of marriage, it is the first letter I have ever received. It began, 'Of course, Buster, you can stay with us. You are an author, not a dog.' The Man always resents any mention of my literary distinction, but yesterday resentment gave way to pleasure as he read on. 'Because of the anxiety we have caused you, we will be pleased to charge you at last year's rate.'

I expected at least a biscuit as a sign of gratitude, but all he did was make some calculations on the back of the envelope and say, 'We've saved pounds.' We? Whose name was at the top of the letter?

Edinburgh, 21 August

A long, hot journey to Edinburgh. As usual, The Man got lost in the city's one-way system. Humans have absolutely no sense of direction. Once we had passed Lauder, I could have smelt my way to Princes Street blindfolded.

At the Balmoral, the men who help with the suitcases and bags wear skirts. This could be very upsetting for dogs, as we like to be clear about other animals' gender. However, I can detect testosterone from the distance of half a mile. So, when we got out of the car, there was no need to sniff about. That was just as well. It was a moment when it was vital to protect my dignity.

The men in skirts ignored The Man and said, 'Welcome to the Balmoral, Buster.' The room – bigger than the one we had ordered – was in my name. However, The Man had to sign us in. Apparently, pawprints are unacceptable.

In the room, there was a special bed for me and a drinking bowl marked 'Dog'. Normally I resent being referred to in that way. I have a name and people should use it. But it was clear the Balmoral management wanted to be kind. That was

evident by the plate of dog biscuits next to the plate of 'Highland shortbreads' on the dressing table. Frankly, I would have preferred the shortbreads to the dog biscuits, but I accepted the gift in the spirit in which it was offered.

I could tell by the way he behaved that The Man was going to go out and leave me. The walk up Calton Hill was just an attempt to get me so tired that I slept while he was away. 'Don't worry,' he said, 'the Tattoo does not go on for very long.' He was almost out though the door when he walked back across to the window. 'Better draw the curtains. All the flashing and banging might worry you.'

He always overreacts to flashing and banging. If he had not told me about it, I probably would not have even noticed. But, when the flashing and banging began, my interest had been aroused. All I wanted was to see what was going on. Because the curtains were in the way, I gave them a little tug.

The Balmoral, being a very posh hotel, had very heavy curtains. They were fastened to a very long curtain pole, with very big curtain rings. So my little tug had no effect. So I tugged again a little harder. I forget how many tugs it took to pull the curtains down. But I remember that I was nearly struck a nasty blow by the curtain pole. The window ledge was so high that even when I stood on the pile of curtains, I could not see out. So I went to sleep – not in the special bed but on the pile of curtains.

I was woken up by The Man. If I do not rush at him as he comes in the door, he usually says, 'Very slow.' But last night he behaved strangely instead of waiting for me to rush at him and feeling for a biscuit in his pocket: he just stood and looked at the window. Then he said, 'You've done it this time, Buster' – exactly the words he used on the day the policeman arrested him after I had defended myself against the kamikaze royal goose in St James's Park.

For more than an hour he made feeble attempts to hang the curtains back up again and repeated time after time, 'And they've been so kind to us.' Then he said something silly: 'How could you do it, Buster?' Surely he could have worked this out for himself. I just got hold of the curtains in my teeth and pulled. I was pleased when he said, 'You must be very strong' – even though he sounded like he would have preferred me to be very weak. Then he sat on the bed and stared at the telephone muttering, 'We'll just have to tell the truth.'

I could not quite make out what he said on the telephone, but when it was all finished, he said (very solemnly), 'The Manager is coming up straight away.'

We have a procedure for welcoming guests into our hotel room, but if possible we like to identify them before they ring the bell. That minimises the amount of barking. But, at whatever stage of progress we realise that they are approaching, The Man says, 'Bathroom!' and in I go. The rule applies to the arrival of breakfast, newspapers or The Manager coming up to talk about curtains. Usually I have to stay in until the visitor departs. But last night I was let out almost straight away. A woman, presumably The Manager, scratched me behind the ears and told me that she liked dogs. The Man seemed to have regained his composure and said, as if he had known all along, 'The curtains will be up again when we get back from our walk up Carlton Hill tomorrow morning.'

Fort William, 25 August

We have moved on to Inverlochy Castle Hotel, which The Man – being a snob – says is probably the best hotel in the world. It is so special that the lady at reception said that I could not stay in the bedroom when The Man went down to dinner. For once, The Man was on my side – something that never happens when I confront a cat. 'If that is the case,' he said, 'I must leave at once.'

The Manager, another one, came to see us. I sat and looked innocent while The Man lied on my behalf. 'Buster,' he said, 'can be trusted with anybody and anything. He has stayed at all the best hotels in Scotland. The Balmoral in Edinburgh last week. Not a stain on the carpet. Not a scratch on the furniture.'

I was reprieved and stayed upstairs when he went down to dinner. But a terrible precedent was established. When he left, I was put in the bathroom. The shower curtain was tucked behind the bath taps and the towels were taken into the bedroom. I can look forward to many lonely nights on linoleum floors, watching taps drip and wondering how much damage I can do to a toilet roll.

The next morning I felt poorly. When I am under the weather, my stomach contracts and I start to wheeze. She screamed to The Man, 'Buster's going to be sick. We cannot let him be sick here.'

The Man froze. Then he said, 'Oh, God, I told The Manager he'd never even made a stain on a carpet.' Without any warning, She brutally picked me up, carried me into the bathroom and dropped me in the bathtub. I was stunned. But I was also sick. The Man said, 'Oh, Buster, thank goodness, we got you here in time.' As is often the case, I thought, What does he mean by 'we'? She lifted me and carried me. She who never lifts heavy weights. It just goes to show how much She values other people's carpets.

Derbyshire, 7 September

The village fell race was held earlier this evening – a hundred and fifty men and women running through the hills about as fast as I would go if The Man could keep up with me.

They all start together from the playing fields – 'No dogs allowed except on the footpaths' – after The Man makes a big bang with a machine that is normally used to throw clay pigeons in the air. I have never seen a clay pigeon and cannot imagine how they fly. Perhaps they need a machine that throws them in the air to get them airborne.

I watched from near the gate with Mr Watson, the gardener, and when they all came running past I noticed that one runner had floppy shorts. I do not like floppy shorts. So I had a nip at them. Unfortunately, I missed my target and caught the leg inside. It cannot have hurt very much, for the runner (to whom the leg was attached) squealed, swore and then ran on.

The runner with the floppy shorts won the fell race. When The Man presented him with the cup, he suggested that it was my nip that had got him off to a flying start. The runner with the floppy shorts did not laugh.

London, 10 September

The Man is worried about how I behave in the morning.

When I get up, I stretch a lot, first front legs and then back. That is because my legs are stiff. Even when I stretch, it takes a while for the stiffness to ease off. It looks as though I shall soon be back to the vet. Another needle in my back seems certain.

11 September

The nice new vet. The one who instead of putting me on the table – which I hate – kneels down on the floor. He says that I have something called arthritis. The Man – who hates not to be the centre of attention – says that he has it too. The new vet says that he will give me medicine that will make me 'like a spring chicken again'. I have never been a spring chicken.

Nor do I wish to become one. All I want is not to be stiff in the mornings.

12 September

When we came back from the vet's, The Man complained about the cost of my medicine and tried to make the usual jokes about my being a private patient. I see nothing funny about my getting older.

I am to take glucosamine tablets. I almost choked on the first one. No one told me that it was chewable. So (as is my way) I bolted it. After my coughing fit, She started the 'Oh, Buster. Look. Look. Yum,' in order to fool me into thinking that the tablets are a treat. To make them even more desirable, she makes me 'sit' before I am allowed to have one. The trick has worked. Now when I see the glucosamine tablet being pressed out, I start to salivate.

The Man now insists that I crunch the glucosamine tablet. 'Crunch, Buster. Give me a big crunch.' Sometimes it is difficult to regard him as a serious person.

Derbyshire, 1 October

When we arrived, The Man decided, without even giving me the chance to do my necessary scout round the house, that we would have one of our regular wrestles on the landing in the middle of the stairs. He knows that I like to be higher than he is and so he waits until I have rushed up the stairs and then he pulls a biscuit out of his pocket and moves it from hand to hand. He mocks me when I cannot work out which hand has the biscuit. He knows that I could have his nose off if I wished. But I know that he is my true friend, so I am careful not to snap too close to his face. I always get the biscuit in the end. That may prove that he is my true friend, or it may just show that he cannot fight.

London, 5 October

I do not like sleeping in the hall.

I have decided to make an assault on fortress bedroom.

On my first night with The Man, he expected me to sleep in the utility room on the far side of the kitchen. But I howled until I was moved into the hall just outside the bedroom door. At the time I thought it was a victory. Slowly over the years, I have begun to realise that it was only a very small first step. Being satisfied is not my way. It is essential to my personal esteem that I move out of the hall. More howling is called for.

7 October

Assault timed to begin at midnight – i.e. immediately after I heard him switch off the television. Produce an anguished howl. On hearing me, The Man resorted to shouted threats. I was too tired to continue after five minutes.

9 October

Howled again. The Man came out of the bedroom and knelt down by my basket. After a couple of minutes, he shouted, 'He's all right – just trying it on.' Discouraged, I went back to sleep.

10 October

Realised my mistake. Should have whined, not howled. Whining sounds like real distress. The Man came out of the bedroom more quickly. Stayed longer, rubbing and scratching behind ears. Unfortunately, I went to sleep again. 'If this goes on,' he said, 'we'll have to take him to the vet.'

11 October

Prolonged whining interspersed with sharp barks. The Man came out of the bedroom so quickly that his pyjama trousers fell down. He shouted back to the bedroom, 'Can't be much wrong with him – he's not off his food.' I cannot see what that has got to do with my need to move into the bedroom at night. Then he sat on the floor and said to me, 'You're fine now, Buster, I'm here.' He does not understand that I will not be fine until I move into the bedroom. It is a matter of status.

12 October

Tonight when I started to bark, She said, 'The vet in Sheffield suggested that we drop something near to him. The big bang will bring him to his senses. There are two possibilities – keys or a book. Let's start with keys.'

Keys? Keys play a big part in my life. I can hear keys jangling from twenty yards away. Sometimes the sound of keys means someone is about to leave. At least four times a day, it means that I am about to go out. And that means a biscuit. So, although keys do not smell of biscuits, the sound of keys gets my salivary glands going and I start to dance for joy. The Man says that I am a joyful creature. This is true. I hope that nothing is going to happen with keys to spoil their reputation.

13 October

I had barely given a preparatory howl when She came out of the bedroom and dropped a bunch of keys dangerously near my head. After She had done it three times, he shouted that the noise is worse than my barking. She went back to bed, stuffing bits of foam into her ears. If I did that, we could all be attacked in our beds. I heard her say, 'We'll have to try the dictionary tomorrow.'

14 October

I howled very effectively last night. After only a couple of seconds She came out of the bedroom with a huge dictionary and dropped it right near my head. I could have received a nasty injury. Luckily, the spine broke and She returned to the bedroom nursing the injured book. Still not in the bedroom.

15 October

Decided on shock tactics. Rammed the bedroom door with my head. No damage done to head. The Man out of bedroom faster than on the night when his pyjamas fell down, and said, 'He must be really distressed. If this goes on, we will have to have him in the bedroom – at least for a night or two.' Nearly there.

16 October

The Man is very bad-tempered. I put it down to envy. The medicine given to me by the nice new vet is working. I am ready to chase squirrels again. He is still stiff in the morning and, as far as I can make out, for most of the day. My assaults on the bedroom door have not improved his humour.

The arthritis medicine is not, however, a total blessing. The problem arises at breakfast time. As well as the tablet, drops of medicine have to be sprinkled on my breakfast – my only meal of the day. There was a time when I thought of food as 'sawdust balls' and I longed to live on the rotting rabbits' carcasses that I can smell in the hedgerows and the restaurant refuse on which I was brought up when I was living wild. But after nearly nine years the sawdust balls have become my breakfast of choice. My complaint is not what I get fed but how long it takes to get it. The medicine has lengthened the delay.

Early mornings are frustrating enough as it is. When The Man eventually gets up, instead of taking me on my walk at once, he wanders about reading the newspapers and drinking orange juice. Even when he becomes fully conscious, he insists on getting dressed before he takes me out. Most days, he even shaves and showers. Then he says, 'Ready to go.' But usually we are not. I am. Indeed, I leap about and bark in anticipation of the pleasures in store – defecating, kicking up grass with my back legs in celebration of my invariably regular bowels and having the biscuit that is my reward. But he has to search for his keys, find his mobile, look for my lead and get the essential 'pick-up bag' out of the utility room. Now he also has to collect my glucosamine tablet. It all takes valuable time.

Even when we get back I am not served breakfast immediately. I have to wait until She and The Man have theirs. This is supposed to confirm my place in the pack. But everybody knows what that place is. She is leader. I am second. The Man comes a poor third. But the ritual must be observed.

Fortunately, The Man is a messy eater. So I sit under the table and collect his crumbs as they bounce off his knees and stomach. It is all that stops me going mad. Then I have to 'wait' – as sternly instructed – in my bed, while what ought to be a simple breakfast is prepared.

On the bad days it begins with washing my bowl. That is worse than a waste of time. I would much prefer my bowl to be dirty. Though, to be fair, hand-washing does have one advantage over dishwashing at night: the bowl does not smell of soap. The measuring out of the sawdust balls is, when done by She, absolutely agonising. For She does it with great care. The Man just slops them into the bowl. I prefer slopping. That way I get more.

17 October

Three nights of head-banging have done the trick. Last night I lay in my basket, right up against the wardrobe down under the exercise bicycle, which The Man never uses. Very little sleep, as he snored. And he got up several times in the night and stumbled out of the bedroom. He fell over me every time.

25 October

Late waking up. The Man already in bathroom and bedroom curtains open. Sun streaming in. Stretched by habit, although arthritis nearly gone. Felt lucky to be alive, so I did my happiness roll. Head on floor with bottom in air followed by a quick sideways flip on to my back with legs in air. I also do a special growl at the same time. The Man came out of the bathroom with soap on his face and asked nobody in particular, 'Is there a lion roaring in my bedroom?' Really he knew it was me. He meant that my happiness roll makes him happy too.

1 November

The renewed vigour – brought on by the arthritis medicine – has revived controversy over my barking, which has increased of late.

She claims that I am going deaf and that I bark to prove that even if I hear very little noise, I can make it. This is not true. I bark because, over the years, I have come to realise that barking is one way to get what I want. Barking is only one item in my repertoire of usual sounds. Although it is the loudest, it is not as effective as whining, whimpering and crying. But it is much more fun.

When I was a pup I used to howl a lot. I howled on my first night with The Man when he expected me to sleep in the utility room. I howled every time I was left on my own, and I howled if, even by mistake, I was shut out of the room in which She and The Man were sitting. Now I have put away childish things. All the other noises have better results.

I am a subtle whiner. The Man says, in praise of my doubt-less courage, that every other dog he knew whined when somebody trod on its tail – an unhappily frequent occurrence with domestic animals. I never whine on such occasions. I try to whine with greater discrimination. When it is time for me to go for my evening walk and The Man says, 'I'll just watch *Newsnight* first,' a whine always produces the required result. 'Listen,' She says. 'He really *needs* to go.'

It has to be admitted that, sometimes, I misjudge the whin-ing moment or even wander round whining pointlessly. 'What a baby you are, Buster,' The Man always says. But although he means to be insulting, I do not mind. I have got myself noticed, which is one of the objects of noise of every sort. And, if he were honest, he would admit that he likes me being a baby.

Whimpering, which is only a prolonged and subdued whining, has to be employed with care. Whimper for too long and with too much conviction and there is the real risk of a visit to the vet. Barking, on the other hand, can be absolutely indiscriminate. It is hard to think of a situation when barking is not appropriate.

Barking came to me late in life. During my first six months with The Man I was Buster the Silent. Then, sitting with him on the sofa watching *Coronation Street*, a voice inside my head said, 'Bark.' It was the response to a doorbell – not ringing in our house, but ringing in the television set. Normally I take no notice of television. I can neither see nor hear what is going on. But, on that night, the bell rang loud and clear. I have reacted violently to doorbells ever since.

Derbyshire, 5 November

A big bang in the night. Normally I do not bother about fireworks. But – perhaps because I was half awake – I bothered about that one. The Man did not wake. So I went to the bed and pawed at him. He woke then.

The Man has an obsession with bowels, so he took it for granted that I needed to go out. There was a lot of mumbling while he pulled on his trousers and put a pullover on top of his pyjamas. He then put his sockless feet into his shoes. I think he must have been still half asleep. He put my lead on before he opened the kitchen door. Normally the garden is the one place in which I am allowed my freedom.

Of course I ate grass. It is not very good grass in the garden – very short and a very insipid taste. But any grass is better than none. And grass calms my nerves as well as settles my stomach. Naturally The Man thought that my eating grass confirmed his diagnosis. Then another firework exploded with an even bigger bang than the one that had woken me up. I howled so loudly that even The Man realised what was causing the problem. 'Let's go back in,' he said.

His idea – good in principle – was that we should both sleep in the upstairs drawing room at the front of the house and as far away from the fireworks as possible. He even invited me to share his settee. But he is too big for comfortable cohabitation and too heavy to be pushed off with my back feet. So I went off to a settee on my own. The Man called me an 'ungrateful pig'. Really he knows I am an ungrateful dog.

I proved it by pacing about and whining. Having quickly forgotten about the fireworks – as is my nature – I wanted to go back into the bedroom. The Man followed, but because I could still not settle down, he went to sleep on the floor next to my bed. His arm was on me and my front leg was on him. He stayed there until my snoring became intolerable. I was sorry to feel him go.

10 November

Heard them talking about my ears. At first I feared that they were going to squirt in them again – even though I had not been scratching. Then I realised that they were going on again about me going deaf. The Man is. So he thinks I ought to be. They are still convinced that it is the reason for my loud and continual barking.

I bark a lot – as is my duty. The Man told me about Cerberus at the gate and all that, and although I have only one head, I decided to make enough noise for ten. 'They shall not pass.' That is my motto. At least, they shall not pass without me making a mighty fuss about it. Of course, once a visitor is inside the house, I roll about on my back in the hope that they might scratch my stomach, say, 'What a charmer!'

and give me the biscuit that The Man has passed to them in the mistaken belief that I did not notice.

I have discovered that delivered in the right tone and at the correct moment, a bark becomes a demand. So in Derbyshire I bark when The Man is slow to get up and take me for my walk, and in London I bark when She wastes time in the bathroom instead of getting my breakfast. You can never be quite sure how either of them will react – which is very bad because dogs like consistency. Sometimes they smile and say, 'Listen – Buster is actually talking to us, telling us what he wants.' At other times they get haughty and say, 'Don't give me orders. You know the rules. Back to your bed.' The Man has even been known to say, 'Shut up.' There is, however, one form of barking towards which their attitude never changes. They always hate it. They call it 'pointless barking'.

Now The Man has decided that I wander about barking at nothing in particular because I am going deaf. It saddens me that he understands so little about me – for so-called 'pointless barking' is not pointless at all. It invariably attracts attention. And attention is, after biscuits, what I like most of all. I bark louder than before because, these days, I sometimes cannot hear them when they call and barking also reassures me that we are all still in contact with each other. But I am not going deaf. I just find it harder to hear than I used to.

London, 11 November

Last night, while they were both out, the urge to pull down curtains came upon me again. So I had a tug at the long curtains that hang in front of the steel gate. They fell to the floor at once – which was not very satisfying. Tugging and tearing, over a long period, is much more enjoyable.

When they returned home, The Man was totally unreasonable. What was worse, he gave a demonstration of the inconsistency that dogs hate. Years ago, I tore up the carpet in the hall while they were out. At first The Man was horrified. But then he said, 'Well done, Buster. We would never have dared to risk it in case the mosaic was all broken and cracked. But it's fine. Have a biscuit.' But that is not at all how he reacted to my second attempt to improve the hall. I was made to sit down and listen to a lecture while She kept saying, 'Look at him. He knows he's guilty. He knows that he has done something wrong.' This was true.

12 November

She has persuaded The Man to telephone a 'canine behaviourist'. When I was a pup, canine behaviourists were called dog trainers. The lady behaviourist has told him how to get me out of the bedroom and back into the hall. He is to move my bed a few inches towards the door every day. If I do not notice, I shall be out in the hall without realising it. They must think I am stupid.

13 November

Bed moved a foot towards the door. No objection to this location, but The Man fell over me more than usual during the night.

20 November

Bed now at side of, rather than bottom of, The Man's bed. Ideal position from my point of view. If only I was a foot or so higher in the air, I would be on equal terms.

23 November

Difficult for The Man to close the bedroom door. Bed in way. But I am still in the bedroom.

24 November

Bed out in the hall.

Waited for The Man to go to sleep. Then barked, howled, whimpered and banged my head against the door. Within five minutes I was back in the bedroom right up against the wardrobe door and under the exercise bicycle he never uses.

All The Man could think of to say was, 'It's the only way to get any sleep.' I reckon I am in the bedroom to stay.

25 November

The more I think about it, the more surprised I am that The Man does not want me to sleep in his bedroom. When I am there, he can wake up to the sight of me rolling on my back to show how pleased I am to be alive. I do it every morning.

27 November

More new rules. My bed is going to be brought into bedroom only after I have been groomed, had my teeth cleaned and been given my green breath sweet. Then She is going to say, 'Wait,' and I have to stand outside and wait until my bed has been placed in its appointed place. The Man complains that 'The dog is being subjected to unreasonable restraints.' How little he understands about pack order. I do not mind waiting for the leader of the pack to take precedence – only him.

Mornings are now much trickier. As soon as I poked my head out of the bedroom door, my bed was thrown into the hall. After my usual second sleep, I wandered about a bit, but She said, 'Buster, you know the rules. Only in the bedroom at night.'

Derbyshire, 1 December

The Man's disloyalty never ceases to amaze me. Today he betrayed me in the most humiliating circumstances. Zoë, my friend who comes to our house in Derbyshire almost every morning and sometimes takes me for a walk, has two Jack Russells. One, naturally enough, is called Jack. Neither of them plays according to the rules. The Man and I go past their house each morning we are in Derbyshire. They both rush to the gate – falling over each other in their anxiety to get there first – and make a terrible noise. I just walk past as if I have not noticed. They have every right to defend their territory, as I would mine. I would despise them if they behaved any differently.

But this morning we met on the road and they both had a nip at me. That is what I meant about breaking the rules. The Man behaved as if he were very angry. Really he was only frightened that I would kill one of them. He held my front half up in the air so that I could not get my teeth into their necks. He need not have worried. Zoë is my friend and her dogs are safe with me. I was just sorry that she did not see The Man support me in all circumstances.

10 December

Tearing things down has become an obsession. Yesterday

afternoon I pulled the curtains from their rail above the front door, and this morning I detached all the coats from the hooks in the back hall. To be honest, that is not quite true. I detached all the coats except The Man's old tweed jacket. Because that was hung by the collar – instead of by the little loop of tape – it would not come off the hook, no matter how hard I pulled. The best I could do was tear off one of the sleeves.

When they both came back, I ran about wildly to demonstrate guilt and make sure that they did not express too much anger. The Man put on the coat with the tattered sleeve and said that he looked like Charlie Chaplin in *City Lights*. Then She was angrier with The Man than she was with me. 'You're encouraging him,' She said. 'Why not give him a biscuit as a sign of approval?' That seemed a good idea to me. But The Man took no notice.

The really bad thing about yesterday was what they said afterwards. 'When we go out, we'll have to take all the coats out of the back hall and shut him out of the front of the house.'

29 December

I have been the victim of a very dirty trick. As predicted, the day came when She went out first and left The Man to put me in the kitchen when he followed. Of course, I refused to go. First he put on his masterful voice, which, frankly, is just a joke. Then he got hold of my collar and began to drag me through the hall. I stuck my legs out, and, as always, he stopped pulling in case he hurt me. He has never learned that the prizes go to the strong.

Back on the half-landing, cleaning my paws with the contentment that comes from the pleasure of victory, I suddenly heard the larder door click open. Whenever that happens, I am drawn by an irresistible force towards whoever is in there among the food. So off I trotted only to find The Man with his hand deep inside a box of biscuits.

I am not allowed in the larder. So I waited patiently for him to come out and duly received my reward. Then he threw two biscuits to the far end of the kitchen. Naturally I pursued them. But I had barely swallowed the first when I heard the door between the front and back of the house slam shut.

You would think he would be ashamed to act in so deceitful a fashion. But he was not. I heard him boasting about it afterwards.

London, 20 March 2005

The people at the GPO sorting office are very stupid. For the second time a 'Special Instruction' meant only for the postman has been left in a bundle of letters. The message on one side was not about us. It said, 'Keep back/Do not deliver. Mrs J. Clarke of 62 Coburg Close is awaiting redirection.' Poor Mrs Clarke. I would hate to be redirected.

Leaving another 'Special Instruction' in our bundle was not the most stupid thing the sorting office did. The message, which was meant for us, made no sense. 'Dog!' (which is true) was followed by a warning: 'Caution – they put a grille across inside when they open the door.' Why do postmen have to be cautious about the grille? And, since there is a grille, why do they have to be cautious about me?

Holyhead, 5 June

We are going to Ireland. I am going to write about a dog's holiday for the *Daily Mail*. At the last minute we nearly did not go. The Man wanted me to travel with him in the boat, sitting under his table. But Irish Ferries would not agree. In the end, he said I could stay on the back seat of the car, so long as the car was locked and he could visit me during the journey. That was against the rules, but Irish Ferries allowed the visits so long as a crew member accompanied The Man to make sure he did not steal anything or let people's car tyres down. If he did visit me during the journey, I did not know about it. He claims I was asleep.

A ferry employee met us in Dublin. He was very offensive. He tapped his nose and said to The Man, 'You haven't fooled me – you wrote the diaries, not the dog.' The Man seemed to be struggling to think how to reply.

Slane, County Meath, 6 June

When we arrived at Rossnaree House, an Irish wolfhound (just like Brendon Bracken from our village) and a sheepdog of some sort bustled up to the car. Fortunately, the natives were friendly. There were fifteen feral cats in the stables, but, although it was supposed to be my holiday, I was not allowed to go anywhere near them. There was also a fat black pig in the kitchen garden. It was tethered to a post by a rope, which was tied round its belly. The Man took me to see the pig. He said, 'You can look but must not touch.'

Belle Island Castle, County Fermanagh, 8 June

All our walks were spoilt by the presence of two intruders whom, I fear, The Man encouraged. One was a middle-aged Labrador who, because of his funny walk, was called Del Boy. The other – a foundling like me but not so handsome – was called Rodney. The Man explained that these names were somehow related to a television programme. But, as I can never see anything on screen, I had no idea what he was talking about.

The Man rather took to Rodney, who developed the irritating habit of starting off with us on our walks and then – being free from the lead that restricts me – in racing ahead. He would leap over obstacles like an Olympic hurdler, make diversions into fields to annoy cattle and then race back with a smug look on his face that said, 'Aren't I clever?' By the end of our stay, I so resented his behaviour that when I saw him running free at the front of the hotel, I chewed a small hole in the bedroom curtain.

Rossnowlagh, County Donegal, 10 June

Clichés come easily to The Man, so there was much talk of 'stretches of golden sand'. I hate sand. It gets between my toes. I also hate the Lough beaches. Armies of students are employed to pick up the litter, so there is hardly anything worth sniffing. And what is a holiday without a good sniff? There is also a problem with the water. When you drink it, it tastes of salt.

Drumcliff, County Sligo, 12 June

It seems we have come all this way just to see a gravestone. It belongs to a man called Yeats. The Man kept reading what the gravestone said.

> *Cast a cold eye*
> *On life, on death.*
> *Horseman, pass by!*

After he had read it about ten times, he asked me, 'What about that, then?' He did not expect a reply. He then said, 'Urinate on the gravestone and you are dead.' He did not mean it.

We drove on to Lough Gill. There is an island in the middle called Innisfree, which I think was the real reason The Man agreed to come to Ireland. However, he did not get to see it. Dogs are not allowed on the boat. The Man would not risk me staying on my own in the car. He was very good about it. He said, 'If I have to choose between you, Buster, and Yeats, you win every time.'

9 December

It seems we are approaching my tenth birthday. There is much talk about the anniversary, but no suggestion of a celebration. The Man actually said that the idea of a party or presents would be ridiculous. 'I admit we spoil Buster. But we spoil him as a dog, not a little man in a fur suit. That's why we don't feed him at the table or let him sleep in our beds.' He then added, in a superior sort of way, 'The Queen feeds her dogs at the table.'

Instead of talking about a celebration, they went on to talk about how I had changed over the years. They had an argument about it.

'He's always been white round his muzzle,' said The Man.

'But not as much,' She told him.

The Man got out a picture of me when I was young – the one of me licking his face that is always being published in the newspapers. It was clear, even to me, that I am whiter than I used to be. But The Man denied it. I think he has a problem facing up to old age.

11 December

Somebody remembered my birthday. Today I got a card and toy from a lady who had read my book. I was not allowed to play with the toy because The Man said that it was dangerous. 'He'll tear it to pieces and choke on the bits,' he said. 'Just like he did with the stuffed rat years ago.' I cannot remember the stuffed rat. Perhaps I *am* getting old. If his attitude towards my toy is anything to go by, The Man certainly is.

Derbyshire, 14 May 2006

More trouble with the garden. A cat seems to have taken up residence in a border above the croquet lawn. But, instead of letting me deal with it, The Man actually makes me wait in the kitchen until he is sure that it has taken refuge over the garden wall. It has nothing to fear from Angus. He only catches dead pheasants and partridges.

The cat is not the main source of my irritation. A new sort

of animal has appeared in the garden. He* is called Frog, and, for some reason, I do not want to catch him. Frog walks very slowly. Sometimes he does not move at all. I could catch him very easily. But something inside tells me to leave him alone.

Frog comes out of the space between the house and garden where The Man keeps wood and coal. I do not go into that space as it is very wet. But Frog seems to like it in there. The Man is very friendly towards Frog. He picks him up every time he comes into the garden and talks to him as if he were a dog. 'It's too dry out here. You'll die. Let's put you some-where where it's wet and you're safe.' I do not like Frog and wish he would go away instead of keep coming back. Sometimes Frog comes and stands by the kitchen door. Anything else would die, but a voice inside me tells me to leave Frog alone. That is very strange. I could easily bite his head off.

She likes Frog no more than I do. When The Man asks her to pick it up, she always refuses. And She talks as if there were a lot of them. I watch them carefully – take it from me, there is only one. Otherwise I would tell the difference. And every time it comes out into the garden, it is exactly the same.

* I assume he is male. With Frog, it is very hard to be sure.

16 May

The Man and She have had an argument about me. The Man thinks I should be allowed to choose the route of my long afternoon walk. She says that I should go the way I am told. She never takes me on my long walk alone. So I go the way I choose.

The problem arises because I always choose to walk down Main Street, turn up Church Lane and later make my way home through the churchyard. The route itself is not the problem. The problem is what I do along the way.

Since what I do along the way is the reason we go for the walk, you would imagine that nobody complains as long as it is done. But The Man complains every time – well, every time I do it in the flowerbed outside Church Lane Farm or in the churchyard. That is because of what follows when the deed is done.

While The Man is 'picking up' – wielding his plastic bag with the dexterity that comes from 'picking up' four times every day for ten years – I am busy kicking up the ground with my back legs. It is an expression of the joy that follows defecation. An emotion that he seems incapable of appreciating. He just complains about damage done to the flowerbed and the churchyard grass. When he complains about this, She always says, 'What did I tell you? You should make him go up the road.'

The Lake District, 1 June

We are on one of those paid holidays. This time it is the Lake District, wherever that may be. As always on these occasions it began with a long car drive – with me strapped on the back seat. Fortunately, I was asleep by the time we left our village.

The Lake District is more water than land, which is no good for dogs – especially dogs who are not natural swimmers. I have known Labradors who were only happy when they were wet. For me, the only good thing about being wet is getting dried and then having a biscuit.

2 June

The ride on the boat was better than I expected. It would have been better still if The Man had not been ashamed of me.

We sat right in front, which The Man – who likes to sound like an expert on everything – called the bows, even though there were no trees. It got very cold and the other people in the bows went inside what The Man called the cabin. We stayed out and shivered.

A kind lady who recognised me came out of the cabin and said, 'There's still room inside.'

The Man told her, 'I don't think I can come in with the dog.' The dog! I have a name and I expect him to use it.

Ten minutes later a sailor came out of the cabin and said, 'Bring him in, if you want to.' By 'him', he meant me.

'Are you sure?' The Man asked.

'Sure,' said the sailor. 'There are a couple of dogs in there already.' That did it.

'Better stay out here,' he said. We shivered for the rest of the trip.

4 June

We have just been for a walk by a lake. We went so near to the water that my feet splashed in the shallow bit at the edge. I like it. Lake District water is better than sea. It does not taste salty. 'I wonder if you can swim,' The Man said. 'Shall I throw you in and see?' I do not know why he says stupid things he does not mean. They are always the same – beating me, giving me away, starving me to death or feeding me to crocodiles. He thinks it is funny. I just find it boring.

Derbyshire, 18 June

We are having more trouble with 'picking up' – an activity that I have always found distasteful. When I was young, I used to make it as difficult for The Man as I could, in the hope I could persuade him to stop. But even though I squatted under bushes, backed up against railings and sat amongst clumps of shrubs, he always followed me with a plastic bag on his hand.

I have now given up even attempting to remedy his perversion. But this morning he descended to new depths of depravity. He has started to examine the plastic bag's contents.

This, he claims, is because the vet has told him that they provide an indication of my state of health. When I did it this morning, he said, 'It's like *The Madness of King George.*' Is it possible that somebody follows King George with a black paper bag and looks inside? I am not sure who King George is. King Charles is, I know, a spaniel. But King George is new to me.

4 July

Frog has a brother. He is big and black, and he came to our door last night. His name is Toad.

2 August

There are times when I think that The Man does it on purpose. Although he has slowed down – mentally and physically – the way he behaved last night can only be a calculated attempt to drive me to hysteria.

After the late walk we are supposed to prepare for bed. But The Man wandered around – switching the television on and off, filling the kettle and then deciding not to boil it, wondering if his shoes needed cleaning but not cleaning them. Then, at last, I heard the scraping noise as a chair was pulled back from the kitchen table. Then my toilette should begin. Often it does not. Tonight it was worse than usual.

I was actually there, standing on my hind legs with my front paws on his knees in the regulation position when he decided to clean the dead hairs out of my brush. So down I went until the job was done. It took about five minutes and then I was back up in my rampant position. I enjoy being brushed but not as much as I enjoy having my teeth cleaned.

My passion for teeth cleaning is unrelated to dental hygiene. I like the taste of the toothpaste. At the moment it is 'beef' – which is fine, though I much prefer 'ripe game'. Anyway, I like 'beef' enough to salivate when he took my toothbrush out of my washbag (which we take on our travels). Last night I told myself to keep calm while he fumbled with the lid of the toothpaste container, but we had not got that far when he stared at the bristles in the brush and said, 'Down again, Buster. We need to do a bit of cleaning here as well.'

Off he went to the sink, where he boiled the kettle. Hot water was poured on my toothbrush and the bristles were squeezed until old diluted toothpaste ran down the sink – completely wasted. By the time he was ready to push the toothbrush into my mouth, I had lost interest in the whole business. So I had to be attracted back into the kitchen and persuaded to resume my precarious position against his knees. Cunningly, The Man opened the packet of toothpaste and waved it in my direction, in the belief that I will find the pungent smell irresistible. I always do.

The Man then forgot all about my nightly green breath sweet. So he said, 'Time for bed, Buster. Night, night.' That is one of the many phrases I always recognise and one of the few instructions from him that I always obey. So I tripped lightly away in the direction of the stairs. But I had barely reached the hall when he called out, 'Back, Buster. I've forgotten the breath sweet.'

The administration of the breath sweet is a ritual just like the arthritis tablet. Almost everything that The Man and I do is. He broke a tablet out of the plastic wrapper and said, 'Now then, Buster. Let's hear a big crunch.' He has not heard a big crunch for five years, because I have not made one. I gave up big crunching when we changed from big yellow breath sweets (which I could catch between my teeth) to little green breath sweets (which get lost in my mouth). So I swallowed it down in one gulp.

After all the fuss and bother, I no longer wanted to go to bed and I took up one of my daytime positions on the half-landing, ready to repel front-door intruders and, at the same time, keeping an eye on the first floor of the house. The Man is always astounded by my conduct and says, 'Buster!' as if he is surprised that I behave in exactly the same way as on the previous night and on several hundred nights before then. Then he says the magic words again: 'Time for bed, Buster. Night, night.' He did it last night and off I went, leaving him to search for his lost spectacles, his missing mobile and his mislaid diary.

20 August

You would not believe their latest idea. I am to be provided with a 'refuge' when they go out. It is in the wine cupboard under the stairs. It is to be made available whenever they go to watch a football team called Sheffield Wednesday. Along with Darren Gough, Mick Hucknall and a nun who supports Newcastle, I appeared in a television advertisement with a Wednesday scarf round my neck in a rakish way. I was the only person in the advertisement who barked.

When Wednesday are at home, there is a lot of rushing, so that they are not late. The Man talks about not wanting to leave me and carefully calculates how long I can be left on my own. But he still goes and I am imprisoned in the kitchen. Recently all the coats have been moved into the utility room before I am shut in and the oven gloves are taken off their hooks. Anything that I might enjoy tugging is wilfully removed. Now the wine-cupboard door is to be left open.

The Man has decided on this crazy scheme after taking advice. This is usually a bad sign, but on this occasion he sought out Mr Poulter from the Mountain Rescue, who always talks a lot of sense. The Man now brings down my upstairs bed and takes it into the kitchen and puts my day bed into the cupboard under the stairs, where the freezer lives. When I am distressed by lightning, I go under tables, so Mr

Poulter suggested that The Man should give me a place where I feel that my back is secure. The noise of the freezer humming sends me to sleep. The truth is that as soon as they leave, I go to sleep – normally in the kitchen, not in the wine cupboard under the stairs. I do not get up until they return, when I always have a celebratory drink of water. My appreciation of time is not very accurate. She knows this, but I do not want The Man to know, as I like him to feel guilty about going out without me.

23 August

Another one of those embarrassing episodes in which The Man pretends to be a dog. I think he would be a dog if he could, but – since he has neither the physique nor the talent – I would much prefer it if he did not expect me to indulge his fantasies.

This evening he got down on all fours and said, 'All right then, Buster, fight me.' I thought it best to ignore him. But he kept nudging me, shoulder to shoulder. In the end I patted him with a paw to show willing and rolled over on to my back, hoping that he would scratch my stomach and thus restore the proper relationship between man and dog.

Instead, he cried, 'Buster's surrendering! Buster's surrendering!' That irritated me. So, when he added, 'I wonder what he'd do if I rolled on my back,' I showed him. He had hardly landed when I was on top of him, front paws on his shoulders and my mouth wide open. He immediately stopped being a dog and cried, in what he thinks is the voice of authority, 'Sit, Buster. Sit.' Had I obeyed immediately, I would have sat on his stomach, which is mostly very wobbly. So I did not move. The Man put his hands on my shoulder and pushed me away. I have never seen him get up so quickly.

London, 24 August

How brief is fame. For the first time I understood how The Man feels being a 'has-been'. She took me to the Cheese Man in Tachbrook Street. The Cheese Man is our friend because he supports Sheffield Wednesday. And he offered me a taste of Irish Emmental. Stilton is actually my favourite, but I knew to keep this to myself as She would only ask how I knew. Of course, She would not let me have the Irish Emmental. Instead, I was given a low-fat biscuit.

On the way out, a young lady asked, 'Is this Ernest?'

'No, this is Buster,' She said. We were both shocked that I was not recognised.

Imagine my surprise when we then saw a brindle Staffordshire bull terrier walking without a lead, just padding down Francis Street behind his lady, who, knowing a celebrity when she sees one, asked, 'Is it Buster?' Then she enquired, 'Is Buster good with other dogs?'

She answered with a question. 'It depends. Has yours been done?'

The lady replied, 'When he was a pup.' And then I was allowed to cross the road.

The lady, who is an artist called Kate, introduced me to the brindle gentleman. At first I barked a lot to make sure Ernest knew who was the alpha male. The artist said that when she and Ernest go to Green Park and walk in front of the palace, the policeman respectfully enquires if she is with Buster. Now I could hardly be confused for Ernest – though the artist said that The Man had once stopped his car and demanded to know who was walking his dog. Ernest is my height (which is unusual for a Staffie), but as The Man's tailor would say, he has a fuller figure – no waist. And not having an Alsatian father, his ears are half pricked as a Staffie's should be, but his tail is long and thin, while mine is full and clearly one of my good features. Again from my father's side, I have a handsome head and good feet. Ernest's toes are turned inwards like pure Staffordshire bull terrier. And he has an usual tiger brindle coat – stripes. I fear that he is a pure-bred, but I will try not to hold it against him.

I never thought I would like to say those words. Companionship at last! I am approaching my eleventh birthday and Ernest is my first friend. The Man (who is jealous of any life I have of my own) dismissed it all, saying that I have no small talk. This is true. I am interested in the big picture. Had I had time, I would have told Ernest about the rat I saw in Greencoat Place. The Man would not let me dispatch it. He said I would get the bubonic plague.

My friend shares my interests. He is interested in sniffing and putting his head in holes. In London we have to make do with drains. Ernest is not very territorial, which is strange, but he clearly enjoys his food. This bodes well. I have been invited for tea.

When we got home, She told The Man about my new acquaintance and asked, 'Do you think that Buster and Ernest will soon be meeting for lunch at the Garrick?' The Man did not laugh.

25 August

The Man is jealous of me. He does not like me to have a life of my own. He is getting more difficult with the garden. I like to go on reconnaissance missions in the bushes on the top tier. I can spend hours stalking small animals. I stare very intently, not making a sound or a move. When they come out, I pounce and frighten them. It is great fun and it helps me hone my skills. But after twenty minutes it's 'Where's Buster?' He rattles my dish, and, much as I would like to hold out for an independent existence, I succumb and trot back into the kitchen. It is only when the cat has intruded and is perched on my wall that I keep my resolve. Then The Man drags me in by my collar.

Now The Man is jealous of my friendship with Ernest. He makes jokes, asking if Ernest was found in a handbag. I do not think the aspersion is funny, but I know he does from his self-satisfied look. The Man has said that Ernest cannot come round as I am very territorial. This is true.

My friend is not like me. He likes entertaining and has said that I can have any of his toys and share his broccoli and carrots. I do not fancy these, but the pasta sounds lovely. As The Man is such a messy eater, over the years I have had lots of pasta when it falls under the table. Ernest also gets a lamb chop, but he said there was enough meat on the bone to share.

Ernest was taught not to chase cats and in exchange he has the freedom to walk off the lead. The idea of sharing food and not chasing cats worried me. I feared that I had picked a soft friend, but Ernest is a big chap and cannot wait to go ratting. He says that we are pack animals and that I am an obvious leader while he is one of nature's deputies. I knew I was a shrewd judge of canine character.

Derbyshire, 26 August

They have changed all the rooms about. This is most confusing. For years I have not been allowed to go into the downstairs drawing room and have been held captive in the sitting room when anybody comes to the front door.

Now the downstairs drawing room is a dining room. And the downstairs sitting room is the downstairs drawing room – complete with all the furniture that I am not allowed to jump on.

There is now an upstairs sitting room where once there was a bedroom. I am allowed in that, but the view from the window seat is not what I am used to. And I do not like change. I can see more from upstairs, but it takes too much time to rush into the hall and make a nuisance of myself whenever anything happens of which I disapprove on the village green.

London, 30 August

Today the workmen in Vincent Square called me 'Old-Timer'. It was not a name I recognised, but I knew from their manner that they thought I was past it. The Man wonders if I should have Alsatian 2000. He says this a lot because my muzzle, snout and even my eyebrows have gone white. But like many of his jokes, he is the only one who ever laughs. I do not think growing old is funny, but I am a creature of Nature and I know that all animals grow sleepy when they are old. I hope that I fall asleep for ever before The Man finally nods off.

Derbyshire, 4 September

The change of rooms turned out to be a triumph – for me. It is impossible to keep me out of the downstairs drawing room – not only because I am quick and strong, but because I have to be shut away somewhere when there is a knock at the front door. Otherwise I would greet the visitor with what The Man calls 'natural ebullience'. And sometimes my natural ebullience is expressed with my teeth – not actually biting, but tugging with enthusiastic affection at sleeves and skirt hems. Whatever the reason, I am again victorious. With the exception of the main guest bedroom, the whole house is now mine.

Sheffield, 9 September

I went out to dinner last night and raised £5,000 for the RSPCA. Well, I helped. It was another one of The Man's mistakes. He thought that we were just going to an auction – him to make a speech and me to be on display. But it turned out that there was a dinner first.

The Man wanted to lock me in the car. But She gave him a hard look and said, 'Hardly the sort of thing to suggest to the RSPCA.' She then told him, 'Leave him to me and he will be perfectly well behaved.' My lead was fastened to the leg of her chair. I was perfectly well behaved but received no reward. If I had been tied to The Man's chair, I would not have been perfectly well behaved. But I would have got some food.

London, 22 September

There is nothing that The Man won't do for money – and expect me to do in support of his avarice. This week – believe it or not – he 'taught me to read'.

The *Daily Mail* – one of the newspapers for which he works – had the idea and they sent him a textbook that explained how he was to give me a lesson. It was, of course, American.

It goes without saying that the whole thing was absurd. All I had to do was stare at cards on which The Man had written words. At first he told me what the word was and I did whatever it said. After he had shouted, 'Sit,' a dozen times (and given me a biscuit every time I did it), he stopped shouting and just showed me the card. Of course, I had got into the habit. So I sat down again. On the strength of this performance he wrote two thousand words, 'How I Taught Buster to Read'. I feel that I have been an accessory to a fraud.

Envoi

No doubt you expect my diaries to end with some emotional slush like 'Regrets, I've had a few, but then again, too few to mention.' Not a hope. I didn't do it my way. If I had, I would have eaten more biscuits, menaced more cats and never gone out in the rain. I would have slept on their bed and been fed first and from the table. And I would have been allowed to suck the toothpaste out of the tube instead of having it rubbered on my teeth with a brush.

I did it their way – She and The Man. Sit down! Quiet! Back up! No barks! Come here at once! Wait! Quiet, Buster! That's how I travelled every highway. And, what is more, the end is nowhere near. I am a fit and self-confident eleven-year-old. The years stretch ahead and I have never doubted it.

Well, only once. That is when The Man wrote an article for a newspaper (in my name) on cloning. He told me that it was possible to make another me – exactly the same, only young. For a moment I worried if he would swap me for a newer model. I worry about that no more.

Yesterday we were out for a walk when a person stopped

and said, 'Is that the original Buster?'

The Man was outraged. 'Of course,' he said. 'A little whiter round the jaw. A little fatter round the middle. And a little longer in the teeth that remain. But there is, and always will be, only one Buster.' That is good enough for me.